QUOTABLE
WISDOM

•

Abraham Lincoln

Edited by
CAROL KELLY-GANGI

STERLING
New York

To my brother Tom with love—
whose integrity and honesty I greatly admire.

A special thanks to my parents, Gwen and Howard Kelly; Marianne Kelly; and
Beverly Lindh for sharing not only their books on Lincoln, but their insights as well.
And as always, thanks to my husband, John, for his shared love of history and
for all of his valuable contributions.

STERLING
New York

An Imprint of Sterling Publishing Co., Inc.
1166 Avenue of the Americas
New York, NY 10036

STERLING and the distinctive Sterling logo are
registered trademarks of Sterling Publishing Co., Inc.

Compilation © 2007 by Fall River Press
Originally published in 2007 as *Abraham Lincoln: His Essential Wisdom*

The quotes in this book have been drawn from many sources, and are assumed to be accurate
as quoted in their previously published forms. Although every effort has been made to
verify the quotes and sources, the Publisher cannot guarantee their perfect accuracy.

ISBN 978-1-4549-1121-0

Distributed in Canada by Sterling Publishing Co., Inc.
c/o Canadian Manda Group, 664 Annette Street
Toronto, Ontario M6S 2C8, Canada
Distributed in the United Kingdom by GMC Distribution Services
Castle Place, 166 High Street, Lewes, East Sussex BN7 1XU, England
Distributed in Australia by NewSouth Books
45 Beach Street, Coogee NSW 2034, Australia

For information about custom editions, special sales, and premium and corporate purchases,
please contact Sterling Special Sales at 800-805-5489 or specialsales@sterlingpublishing.com.

Manufactured in the United States of America

10 9

– Contents –

– Introduction –

Born, February 12, 1809, in Hardin County, Kentucky.
Education defective.
Profession, a lawyer.
Have been a captain of volunteers in Black Hawk War.
Postmaster at a very small office.
Four times a member of the Illinois legislature, and was a member
of the lower house of Congress.

— Abraham Lincoln

B ASED ON LINCOLN'S OWN autobiographical entry
written in June of 1858 for the *Dictionary of Congress*, it seems
unimaginable that in less than three years, he would find
himself elected to the office of the President of the United States.
Indeed, in highlighting only the most basic facts from his life,
Lincoln seemed unaware that by June of 1858, he had risen far
above local prominence.

But for a single occurrence that touched off a sequence of events that would ultimately lead Lincoln to the White House, his political life could very well have ended in a more or less lackluster fashion. In the spring of 1849, Lincoln had finished his term in the U.S. House of Representatives and in keeping with a promise he had made to serve only one term, he did not seek reelection. Rather, he returned to Springfield and resumed his law practice. As his reputation for being an excellent lawyer thrived, so did his legal practice. He was representing prestigious clients, including banks, insurance companies, and the powerful Illinois Central Railroad, and he appeared regularly before the Illinois Supreme Court.

His family was also expanding, with Mary giving birth to sons William and Tad after losing son Edward, who died after a two-month illness when only a toddler. Later admitting that his interest in politics was waning at this point, Lincoln may well have slipped back into private life for good.

But on May 30, 1854, an event happened that Lincoln later said "astounded" him leaving him "thunderstruck and stunned." It was also the catalyst that Lincoln needed to re-ignite his interest in politics and eventually focus national attention on him. It was the passage of the Kansas-Nebraska Act, which had been introduced in Congress earlier in the year by Lincoln's longtime political rival, Stephen A. Douglas. The Act allowed the settlers in the territories of Kansas and Nebraska to determine whether or not slavery would be allowed within their borders. It thus rendered the Missouri Compromise of 1820, the longstanding agreement prohibiting the extension of slavery, "inoperative and void." Speaking at a Whig convention later that summer, Lincoln attacked the Act calling it a "great wrong and injustice." For the fifth time, Lincoln was elected to the Illinois State legislature, but declined the seat in order to make a bid for the Senate. Though he lost the Senate race, having thrown his supporters to an anti-Nebraska Democrat to prevent a win by a Douglas-supported Democrat, he continued his course of action in vigorously denouncing the Kansas-Nebraska Act and the extension of slavery at every opportunity—all the while gaining more and more attention, admiration, and supporters.

Within two years, Lincoln would make another bid for the Senate, this time for the seat held by Douglas himself. During the campaign, Lincoln invited Douglas to a series of seven debates in various locations throughout the state. The debates were wildly successful with an average of ten to fifteen thousand people in attendance to hear Lincoln and Douglas in their heated exchange over the issue that was causing a firestorm of controversy in the nation.

Although Douglas won the Senate seat by a slim margin, the debates had served to thrust Lincoln into the national spotlight. In a brilliant political move, Lincoln actively lobbied to have his scrapbook of clippings and major speeches of the debates published in book form in 1860. It became an immediate best-seller. So it was, that within sixteen months of losing the Senate race, Lincoln was nominated as the Republican presidential candidate.

The challenges and seemingly insurmountable odds that Lincoln faced in politics he also faced regularly in other areas of his life. His impoverished beginnings and his family's struggle for survival from their meager crops marked his earliest years. Then, at the age of nine, Lincoln lost his beloved mother, Nancy Hanks

Lincoln. His father, Thomas, remarried a widow with three children, Sarah Bush Johnston, a year later. She proved to be a wonderful choice for Thomas and his family and raised the Lincoln children with love and affection.

Lincoln's self-described defective education consisted of brief stints in log-house schools along with his sister Sarah when he was a boy. He learned to "read, write, and cipher to the Rule of Three; but that was all." The remainder of what he learned, he taught himself "under the pressure of necessity." He read the family Bible—which would provide him with comfort and reassurance for the balance of his life—Shakespeare, and whatever books he could borrow from friends between plowing, planting, and working as a hired hand for neighbors.

Lincoln moved to Illinois with his family in 1830, and made his first known political speech to promote better navigation along the Sangamon River. The following year, he moved to New Salem on his own. He worked as a store clerk, made friends, and gained the respect of the local men, in part after wrestling the leader of a local gang to a draw. In 1832, Lincoln's mettle was further tested in the Black Hawk War, where he was elected the company captain, a success that gave him great personal satisfaction. Later that year, Lincoln ran for the Illinois General Assembly. He lost the election, but it was, as he pointed out, the only time he'd ever been "beaten by the people."

In 1833, Lincoln was left deep in debt after a general store that he'd opened with a partner failed. In need of money, he began writing deeds and mortgages for neighbors and worked as a hired hand. He was later appointed postmaster of New Salem, and then the deputy surveyor for the County. The following year,

Lincoln was elected to the Illinois General Assembly, and began in earnest his study of law. Without the benefit of any higher education or mentors, Lincoln studied Blackstone's *Commentaries* and other law books borrowed from a friend with a single-minded purpose and drive, and greatly sharpened his analytical, reasoning, and interpretive skills in the process.

Lincoln faced yet another devastating loss in 1835. It was then that Ann Rutledge, said to be Lincoln's first love, died from a fever at the age of twenty-two. The two had known each other since 1831 when Lincoln befriended her father, James Rutledge, a local tavern-keeper. What started as friendship between the two, turned to romance, and likely to an engagement. Friends of Lincoln recalled that he fell into a deep depression upon her death, which was the third time he had suffered the loss of a woman close to him, after his mother, and his sister Sarah, who had died in childbirth in 1828.

In the spring of 1837, Lincoln left New Salem for Springfield. He had received his law license the year before and was ready to begin his legal career. He roomed with Joshua F. Speed, who became his lifelong friend, and joined John T. Stuart in a legal partnership. He practiced in the areas of both civil and criminal law, and in 1839, made his first trip on the Illinois Eighth Judicial Circuit. This required Lincoln to travel on horse-back or in horse-drawn carriage from courtroom to courtroom on legal matters all over central and eastern Illinois.

It was also in 1839, that Lincoln met Mary Todd, the daughter of a prominent Kentucky banker, at a local ball. After an on-again off-again relationship that involved a broken engagement and much despair on both sides, the two married quietly in 1842 after secretly resuming their courtship. In 1843, their first son, Robert Todd Lincoln was born. He would be the only of their four sons to reach adulthood. And in 1844, Lincoln started his own practice and took in a young partner, the twenty-six-year-old William H. Herndon. The same year, the Lincolns moved into a house in Springfield purchased for $1,500.00, which was their home until 1861. A second son, Edward, was born in 1846, and on August 3rd, Lincoln was elected to the U.S. House of Representatives.

After his rise to national recognition from the Lincoln-Douglas debates, Lincoln captured the Republican presidential nomination and then the presidency itself, receiving 180 of 303 electoral votes and 40 percent of the popular vote. When Lincoln assumed office in March of 1861, he did so understanding that he confronted a greater challenge than even Washington had faced. But the same qualities that had served him well in life would aid him in the biggest crises in the life of the nation. Scholars point to his steadfast character—molded through a lifetime of adversity—coupled with his political genius, and extraordinary capacity to adapt to new circumstances as key traits that would enable him to successfully lead the country through the Civil War.

Abraham Lincoln: Quotable Wisdom gathers together hundreds of quotations from Lincoln drawn from his letters, speeches, and other writings. In the selections, Lincoln speaks passionately about the paramount need to save the Union; the injustice of slavery and his staunch refusal to compromise over its extension. In letters to his generals and cabinet members he reveals his expert grasp of military matters and his keen understanding of the human psyche. In still other selections he expresses his great affection for his wife and their "dear rascals"; and sincerely consoles those who have lost loved ones in the War.

Of the countless tributes and eulogies that were written in an attempt to make sense out of Lincoln's shocking death, perhaps the words of Noah Brooks, Lincoln's friend and journalist, written more than thirty years after Lincoln's death, do much to express the essence of this extraordinary man and his place in history: "He no longer stands for what is best in American life and genius, but for what is best in humanity. He belongs to the world, not alone to us."

— Carol Kelly-Gangi

– Early Years –

It is a great piece of folly to attempt to make anything out of me or my early life. It can all be condensed into a single sentence, and that sentence you will find in Gray's Elegy, 'The short and simple annals of the poor.' That's my life, and that's all you or anyone else can make out of it.

> — Lincoln's response to John L. Scripps of the *Chicago Tribune* when asked for material to be used in a campaign biography, from *Herndon's Lincoln: The True Story of a Great Life* by William H. Herndon and Jesse W. Weik

Good boys who to their books apply
Will all be great men by and by.

> — Doggerel penned by Lincoln as a youngster for his friend Joseph C. Richardson, from *The Hidden Lincoln: From the Letters and Papers of William H. Herndon* edited by Emanuel Hertz

Abraham Lincoln,
　His hand and pen,
He will be good,
　But God knows when.

> — Doggerel written by Lincoln as a youngster in his
> notebook, from *Herndon's Lincoln: The True Story of a Great
> Life* by William H. Herndon and Jesse W. Weik

My dear Sir:

Herewith is a little sketch, as you requested. There is not much of it, for the reason, I suppose, that there is not much of me. If anything be made out of it, I wish it to be modest, and not to go beyond the material. If it were thought necessary to incorporate anything from any of my speeches, I suppose there would be no objection. Of course it must not appear to have been written by myself.

I was born February 12, 1809, in Hardin County, Kentucky. My parents were both born in Virginia, of undistinguished families—second families, perhaps I should say. My mother, who died in my tenth year, was of a family of the name of Hanks. . . . My father, at the death of his father, was but six years of age; and he grew up, literally without education. He removed from Kentucky to what is now Spencer County, Indiana, in my eighth year. We reached our new home about the time the State came into the Union. It was a wild region, with many bears and other wild animals still in the woods. There I grew up. . . . There was absolutely nothing to excite ambition for education. Of course when I came of age I did not know much. Still somehow, I could read, write, and cipher to the Rule of Three; but that was all. I have not been to school since. The little advance I now have upon this store of education, I have picked up from time to time under the pressure of necessity.

> — Excerpt from short sketch of his life that Lincoln
> wrote at the request of friend and supporter, J. W.
> Fell, for a biographical article, December 20, 1859

I can say this, that among my earliest recollections I remember how, when a mere child, I used to get irritated when anybody talked to me in a way I could not understand. . . . I can remember going to my little bedroom, after hearing the neighbors talk of an evening with my father, and spending no small part of the night walking up and down, and trying to make out what was the exact meaning of some of their, to me, dark sayings. I could not sleep, though I often tried to, when I got on such a hunt after an idea, until I had caught it; and when I thought I had got it, I was not satisfied until I had repeated it over and over, until I had put it in language plain enough, as I thought, for any boy I knew to comprehend.

> — Remark to Reverend J. P. Gulliver, from *Six Months at the
> White House with Abraham Lincoln* by F. B. Carpenter

They got on board, and I lifted up their heavy trunks, and put them on deck. The steamer was about to put on steam again, when I called out that they had forgotten to pay me. Each of them took from his pocket a silver half-dollar, and threw it on the floor of my boat. I could scarcely believe my eyes as I picked up the money. Gentlemen, you may think it was a very little thing, and in these days it seems to me a trifle; but it was a most important incident in my life. I could scarcely credit that I, a poor boy, had earned a dollar in less than a day,—that by honest work I had earned a dollar. The world seemed wider and fairer before me. I was a more hopeful and confident being from that time.

> — Lincoln's remarks to Secretary Seward and others about how he had earned his first dollar, quoted in *Six Months at the White House with Abraham Lincoln* by F. B. Carpenter

My heart lies buried there.

> — Remark to William H. Herndon about the death of Ann Rutledge, Lincoln's first love who died in August of 1835, from *Herndon's Lincoln: The True Story of a Great Life* by William H. Herndon and Jesse W. Weik

Friend Mary:

This thing of living in Springfield is rather a dull business after all, at least it is so to me. I am quite as lonesome here as ever was anywhere in my life. I have been spoken to by but one woman since I've been here, and should not have been by her, if she could have avoided it. I've never been to church yet, nor probably shall not be soon. I stay away because I am conscious I should not know how to behave myself.

I am often thinking about what we said of your coming to live at Springfield. I am afraid you would not be satisfied. There is a great deal of flourishing about in carriages here, which it would be your doom to see without sharing in it. You would have to be poor without the means of hiding your poverty. Do you believe you could bear that patiently? Whatever woman may cast her lot with mine, should any ever do so, it is my intention to do all in my power to make her happy and contented; and there is nothing I can imagine, that would make me more unhappy than to fail in the effort. I know I should be much happier with you than the way I am, provided I saw no signs of discontent in you.

> — Letter to Mary S. Owens, May 7, 1837. Though
> Lincoln was initially ambivalent about his feelings for
> Owens, it was she who finally ended the relationship
> by rejecting his marriage proposal.

Others have been made fools of by the girls; but this can never be with truth said of me. I most emphatically, in this instance, made a fool of myself. I have now come to the conclusion never again to think of marrying; and for this reason; I can never be satisfied with any one who would be block-head enough to have me.

> — Letter to Mrs. Orville H. Browning, explaining his mortification at Mary S. Owens's refusal of his marriage proposal, April 1, 1838

Dear Stuart:

Yours of the 3rd. Inst. is recd. & I proceed to answer it as well as I can, tho' from the deplorable state of my mind at this time I fear I shall give you but little satisfaction. . . . For not giving you a general summary of news, you *must* pardon me; it is not in my power to do so. I am now the most miserable man living. If what I feel were equally distributed to the whole human family, there would not be one cheerful face on the earth. Whether I shall ever be better I cannot tell; I awfully forebode I shall not. To remain as I am is impossible; I must die or be better, it appears to me. . . .

> — Letter to John T. Stuart, Lincoln's law partner, January 23, 1841. Having broken his engagement to Mary Todd weeks before writing this letter, Lincoln fell into a deep depression.

Since then, it seems to me, I should have been entirely happy but for the never-absent idea that there is *one* still unhappy whom I have contributed to make so. That kills my soul. I cannot but reproach myself for even wishing to be happy while she is otherwise.

> — Lincoln's letter to his lifelong friend Joshua F. Speed, referring to his broken engagement with Mary Todd, March 1842

Nothing new here, except my marrying, which to me, is matter of profound wonder.

> — Closing remark in letter to Samuel D. Marshall, November 11, 1842

– Politics –

Fellow-Citizens:

I presume you all know who I am. I am humble Abraham Lincoln. I have been solicited by many friends to become a candidate for the Legislature. My politics are short and sweet, like the old woman's dance. I am in favor of a national bank. I am in favor of the internal improvement system, and a high protective tariff. These are my sentiments and political principles. If elected, I shall be thankful; if not it will be all the same.

> — First Political Speech, Pappsville, Illinois, March 1832.
> Lincoln, aged 23, did not win the election; it was the
> only time he was ever defeated by popular vote.

Every man is said to have his peculiar ambition. Whether it be true or not, I can say for one that I have no other so great as that of being truly esteemed of my fellow men, by rendering myself worthy of their esteem. How far I shall succeed in gratifying this ambition, is yet to be developed. I am young and unknown to many of you. I was born and have ever remained in the most humble walks of life. I have no wealthy or popular relations to recommend me. My case is thrown exclusively upon the independent voters of this county, and if elected they will have conferred a favor upon me, for which I shall be unremitting in my labors to compensate. But if the good people in their wisdom shall see fit to keep me in the background, I have been too familiar with disappointments to be very much chagrined.

— Letter entitled "To the People of Sangamon County," March 9, 1832, while a candidate for the Illinois State Legislature

Considering the great degree of modesty which should always attend youth, it is probable I have already been more presuming than becomes me. However, upon the subjects of which I have treated, I have spoken as I thought. I may be wrong in regard to any or all of them; but holding it a sound maxim, that it is better to be only sometimes right, than at all times wrong, so soon as I discover my opinions to be erroneous, I shall be ready to renounce them.

— Letter entitled "To the People of Sangamon County," March 9, 1832, while a candidate for the Illinois State Legislature

Politicians [are] a set of men who have interests aside from the interests of the people, and who, to say the most of them, are, taken as a mass, at least one long step removed from honest men. I say this with the greater freedom because, being a politician myself, none can regard it as personal.

— Speech before Illinois legislature, January 11, 1837

It would astonish if not amuse, the older citizens of your County who twelve years ago knew me a strange, friendless, uneducated, penniless boy, working on a flat boat—at ten dollars per month to learn that I have been put down here as the candidate of pride, wealth, and aristocratic family distinction.

— Letter to Martin S. Morris, March 26, 1843

My dear Sir:
The election is over, the session is ended and I am not Senator. . . . I started with 44 votes and T. [Trumbull] with 5. It is rather hard for the 44 to have to surrender to the 5 and a less good humored man than I, perhaps, would not have consented to it,—and it would not have been done without my consent. I could not, however, let the whole political result go to smash, on a point merely personal to myself.

— Letter to W. H. Henderson, February 21, 1855

Born, February 12, 1809, in Hardin County, Kentucky.
Education defective.
Profession, a lawyer.
Have been a captain of volunteers in Black Hawk War.
Postmaster at a very small office.
Four times a member of the Illinois legislature, and was a member of the lower house of Congress.

> — Lincoln's sketch of his life provided for the *Dictionary of Congress,* June 1858

Then came the Black-Hawk war; and I was elected a Captain of Volunteers—a success which gave me more pleasure than any I have had since. I went the campaign, was elated, ran for the Legislature the same year (1832) and was beaten—the only time I ever have been beaten by the people. The next, and three succeeding biennial elections, I was elected to the Legislature. I was not a candidate afterwards. During this Legislative period I had studied law, and removed to Springfield to practice it. In 1846 I was once elected to the lower House of Congress. Was not a candidate for re-election. From 1849 to 1854, both inclusive, practiced law more assiduously than ever before. Always a whig in politics, and generally on the whig electoral tickets, making active canvasses. I was losing interest in politics, when the repeal of the Missouri Compromise aroused me again.

> — Autobiographical sketch, December 20, 1859

In this age, and this country, public sentiment is every thing. *With* it, nothing can fail; *against* it, nothing can succeed. Whoever moulds public sentiment, goes deeper than he who enacts statutes or pronounces judicial decisions. He makes possible the enforcement of these, else possible.

> — Notes for Lincoln-Douglas debate at Ottawa, Illinois,
> August 1858

What is conservatism? Is it not adherence to the old and tried, against the new and untried?

> — Speech at Cooper Union, New York City,
> February 27, 1860

I have never had a feeling politically that did not spring from the sentiments embodied in the Declaration of Independence.

> — Address in Independence Hall, Philadelphia,
> February 22, 1861

I distrust the wisdom if not the sincerity of friends who would hold my hands while my enemies stab me.

— Letter to Reverdy Johnson, July 26, 1862

[I feel] somewhat like the boy in Kentucky who stubbed his toe while running to see his sweetheart. The boy said he was too big to cry, and far too badly hurt to laugh.

— Lincoln's reply to question of how he felt about the Democrats winning the New York State elections, quoted in *Leslie's Illustrated Weekly*, November 22, 1862

– The Practice of Law –

I am not an accomplished lawyer. I find quite as much material for a lecture in those points wherein I have failed, as in those wherein I have been moderately successful. The leading rule for the lawyer, as for the man of every other calling, is diligence.

— Notes for a Law Lecture, July 1850

Extemporaneous speaking should be practised and cultivated. It is the lawyer's avenue to the public. However able and faithful he may be in other respects, people are slow to bring him business if he cannot make a speech. And yet there is not a more fatal error to young lawyers than relying too much on speech-making. If any one, upon his rare powers of speaking, shall claim an exemption from the drudgery of the law, his case is a failure in advance.

— Notes for a Law Lecture, July 1850

Resolve to be honest at all events; and if in your own judgment you cannot be an honest lawyer, resolve to be honest without being a lawyer. Choose some other occupation, rather than one in the choosing of which you do, in advance, consent to be a knave.

— Notes for a Law Lecture, July 1850

Dear Sir:
Yours of the 24th, asking "the best mode of obtaining a thorough knowledge of the law" is received. The mode is very simple, though laborious, and tedious. It is only to get the books, and read, and study them carefully. Begin with Blackstone's Commentaries, and after reading it carefully through, say twice, take up Chitty's Pleading, Greenleaf's Evidence, & Story's Equity &c. in succession. Work, work, work, is the main thing.

— Letter to John M. Brockman, September 25, 1860

Dear Sir:
I have just received yours of 16th, with check on Flagg & Savage for twenty-five dollars. You must think I am a high-priced man. You are too liberal with your money. Fifteen dollars is enough for the job. I send you a receipt for fifteen dollars, and return to you a ten-dollar bill.

— Letter to a client, February 21, 1856

An exorbitant fee should never be claimed. As a general rule never take your whole fee in advance, nor any more than a small retainer. When fully paid beforehand, you are more than a common mortal if you can feel the same interest in the case, as if something was still in prospect for you, as well as for your client. And when you lack interest in the case the job will very likely lack skill and diligence in the performance.

— Notes for a Law Lecture, July 1850

Discourage litigation. Persuade your neighbors to compromise whenever you can. Point out to them how the nominal winner is often a real loser—in fees, expenses, and waste of time. As a peacemaker the lawyer has a superior opportunity of being a good man. There will still be business enough.

— Notes for a Law Lecture, July 1850

Dear Sir:

I understand Mr. Hickox will go, or send to Petersburg tomorrow, for the purpose of meeting you to settle the difficulty about the wheat. I sincerely hope you will settle it. I think you *can* if you *will*, for I have always found Mr. Hickox a fair man in his dealings. If you settle, I will charge nothing for what I have done, and thank you to boot. By settling, you will most likely get your money sooner and with much less trouble and expense.

— Letter to a client, February 22, 1850

My Dear Sir:

Yours of the 6th asking permission to inscribe your new legal work to me, is received. Gratefully accepting the proffered honor, I give the leave, begging only that the inscription may be in modest terms, not representing me as a man of great learning, or a very extraordinary one in any respect.

— Letter to William D. Kelly, October 13, 1860

— Government, Democracy, and Country —

Let reverence for the laws, be breathed by every American mother, to the lisping babe, that prattles on her lap—let it be taught in schools, in seminaries, and in colleges;—let it be written in Primers, spelling books, and in Almanacs;—let it be preached from the pulpit, proclaimed in legislative halls, and enforced in courts of justice. And, in short, let it become the *political religion* of the nation; and let the old and the young, the rich and the poor, the grave and the gay, of all sexes and tongues, and colors and conditions, sacrifice unceasingly upon its altars.

— Speech to the Young Men's Lyceum of Springfield,
January 27, 1838

At what point then is the approach of danger to be expected? I answer, if it ever reach us, it must spring up amongst us. It cannot come from abroad. If destruction be our lot, we must ourselves be its author and finisher. As a nation of freemen, we must live through all time or die by suicide.

> — Speech to the Young Men's Lyceum of Springfield,
> January 27, 1838

I am exceedingly anxious that this Union, the Constitution, and the liberties of the people shall be perpetuated in accordance with the original idea for which that struggle was made, and I shall be most happy indeed if I shall be an humble instrument in the hands of the Almighty, and of this, his almost chosen people, for perpetuating the object of that great struggle.

> — Speech to the New Jersey Senate, Trenton, New Jersey,
> February 21, 1861

The legitimate object of government, is to do for a community of people, whatever they need to have done, but can not do *at all*, or can not *so well do*, for themselves—in their separate, and individual capacities.

> — Speech entitled "Fragments on Government," 1854

Must a government, of necessity, be too *strong* for the liberties of its own people, or too *weak* to maintain its own existence?

— Special Message to Congress, July 4, 1861

It appears that if all men were just, there still would be *some*, though not *so much*, need of government.

— Speech entitled "Fragments on Government," 1854

I go for all sharing the privileges of the government, who assist in bearing its burdens.

— Letter to *Sangamon Journal*, June 13, 1836

It is as much the duty of government to render prompt justice against itself, in favor of citizens, as it is to administer the same between private individuals.

— First Annual Message to Congress, December 3, 1861

This country, with its institutions, belongs to the people who inhabit it. Whenever they shall grow weary of the existing government, they can exercise their *constitutional* right of amending it, or their *revolutionary* right to dismember, or overthrow it.

— First Inaugural Address, March 4, 1861

Why should there not be a patient confidence in the ultimate justice of the people? Is there any better or equal hope in the world?

— First Inaugural Address, March 4, 1861

As I would not be a *slave*, so I would not be a *master.* This expresses my idea of democracy. Whatever differs from this, to the extent of the difference, is no democracy.

— Written and signed by Lincoln in the form of an autograph, from *The Wit and Wisdom of Abraham Lincoln* edited by H. Jack Lang

The Democracy of today hold the liberty of one man to be absolutely nothing, when in conflict with another man's right of property; Republicans, on the contrary, are for both the man and the dollar, but in case of conflict the man before the dollar.

— Lincoln's letter in response to group asking him to attend a celebration in honor of Thomas Jefferson's birthday, April 6, 1859

The part assigned to me is to raise the flag, which, if there be no fault in the machinery, I will do, and when up, it will be for the people to keep it up.

— Speech at flag-raising at the Treasury Building, said to be Lincoln's briefest public address, from *The Wit and Wisdom of Abraham Lincoln* edited by H. Jack Lang

It is not merely for today, but for all time to come that we should perpetuate for our children's children this great and free government, which we have enjoyed all our lives.

— Speech to 166th Ohio Regiment, August 22, 1864

It is not my nature, when I see a people borne down by the weight of their shackles—the oppression of tyranny—to make their life more bitter by heaping upon them greater burdens; but rather would I do all in my power to raise the yoke, than to add anything that would tend to crush them. Inasmuch as our country is extensive and new, and the countries of Europe are densely populated, if there are any abroad who desire to make this the land of their adoption, it is not in my heart to throw aught in their way, to prevent them from coming to the United States.

— Speech to Germans at Cincinnati, Ohio, February 12, 1861

There is more involved in this contest than is realized by every one. There is involved in this struggle the question whether your children and my children shall enjoy the privileges we have enjoyed.

— Speech to 164th Ohio Regiment, August 22, 1864

How hard, oh, how hard it is to die and leave one's country no better than if one had never lived for it!

— Remark to William H. Herndon, from *The Hidden Lincoln: From the Letters and Papers of William H. Herndon* edited by Emanuel Hertz

– Freedom, Equality, and Slavery –

If the safeguards to liberty are broken down, as is now attempted, when they have made *things* of all the free negroes, how long, think you, before they will begin to make *things* out of poor white men? Be not deceived. Revolutions do not go backward.

— Speech before first Republican State Convention,
Bloomington, Illinois, May 29, 1836

———

We have before us, the chief material enabling us to correctly judge whether the repeal of the Missouri Compromise is right or wrong. I think, and shall try to show, that it is wrong; wrong in its direct effect, letting slavery into Kansas and Nebraska—and wrong in its prospective principle, allowing it to spread to every other part of the wide world, where men can be found inclined to take it. This *declared* indifference, but as I must think, covert *real* zeal for the spread of slavery, I cannot but hate. I hate it because of the monstrous injustice of slavery itself. I hate it because it deprives our republican example of its just influence in the world—enables the enemies of free institutions, with plausibility, to taunt us as hypocrites—causes the real friends of freedom to doubt our sincerity, and especially because it forces so many really good men amongst ourselves into an open war with the very fundamental principles of civil liberty—criticizing the Declaration of Independence, and insisting that there is no right principle of action but *self-interest.*

— Speech on the Kansas-Nebraska Act at Peoria, Illinois, October 16, 1854

As a nation we began by declaring that "all men are created equal." We now practically read it "all men are created equal, except negroes." When the Know-nothings get control, it will read "all men are created equal, except negroes and foreigners and Catholics." When it comes to this, I shall prefer emigrating to some country where they make no pretense of loving liberty,—to Russia, for instance, where despotism can be taken pure, and without the base alloy of hypocrisy.

— Letter to Joshua F. Speed in which Lincoln voices his opposition to the extension of slavery, August 24, 1855

You know I dislike slavery; and you fully admit the abstract wrong of it.

— Letter to Joshua F. Speed, August 24, 1855

The Autocrat of all the Russias will resign his crown, and proclaim his subjects free republicans sooner than will our American masters voluntarily give up their slaves.

— Letter to George Robertson, August 15, 1855

The slave-breeders and slave-traders, are a small, odious and detested class, among you; and yet in politics, they dictate the course of all of you, and are as completely your masters, as you are the master of your own negroes.

— Letter to Joshua F. Speed, August 24, 1855

If as the friends of colonization hope, the present and coming generations of our countrymen shall by any means, succeed in freeing our land from the dangerous presence of slavery; and, at the same time, in restoring a captive people to their long-lost father-land, with bright prospects for the future; and this too, so gradually, that neither races nor individuals shall have suffered by the change, it will indeed be a glorious consummation.

— Eulogy on Henry Clay, July 6, 1852

No man is good enough to govern another man *without that other's consent.* I say this is the leading principle—the sheet anchor of American republicanism.

— Speech on the Kansas-Nebraska Act at Peoria, Illinois, October 16, 1854

Those who deny freedom to others deserve it not for themselves.

— Letter to H. L. Pierce, April 6, 1859

Slavery is founded in the selfishness of man's nature—opposition to it is his love of justice. These principles are an eternal antagonism; and when brought into collision so fiercely, as slavery extension brings them, shocks, and throes, and convulsions must ceaselessly follow. Repeal the Missouri Compromise—repeal all compromises—repeal the declaration of independence—repeal all past history, you still can not repeal human nature. It still will be the abundance of man's heart, that slavery extension is wrong; and out of the abundance of his heart, his mouth will continue to speak.

> — Speech on the Kansas-Nebraska Act at Peoria, Illinois, October 16, 1854

Stand with anybody that stands *right*. Stand with him while he is right and *part* with him when he goes wrong.

> — Speech on the Kansas-Nebraska Act at Peoria, Illinois, October 16, 1854

He [Douglas] finds the Republicans insisting that the Declaration of Independence includes ALL men, black as well as white; and forthwith he boldly denies that it includes negroes at all, and proceeds to argue gravely that all who contend it does, do so only because they want to vote, and eat, and sleep, and marry with negroes! He will have it that they cannot be consistent else. Now I protest against that counterfeit logic which concludes that, because I do not want a black woman for a *slave* I must necessarily want her for a *wife*. I need not have her for either, I can just leave her alone. In some respects she certainly is not my equal; but in her natural right to eat the bread she earns with her own hands without asking leave of any one else, she is my equal, and the equal of all others.

— Speech in response to Stephen A. Douglas's defense of the Dred Scott Supreme Court decision, June 26, 1857

I leave you, hoping that the lamp of liberty will burn in your bosoms until there shall no longer be a doubt that all men are created free and equal.

— Speech at Chicago, Illinois, July 10, 1858

All I ask for the negro is that if you do not like him, let him alone. If God gave him but little, that little let him enjoy.

— Speech at Springfield, Illinois, July 17, 1858

———✧———

In their enlightened belief, nothing stamped with the Divine image and likeness was sent into the world to be trodden on, and degraded, and imbruted by its fellows.

— Speech at Lewistown, Illinois, August 17, 1858

———✧———

I was not very much accustomed to flattery, and it came the sweeter to me. I was rather like the Hoosier, with the gingerbread, when he said he reckoned he loved it better than any other man, and got less of it. As the Judge had so flattered me, I could not make up my mind that he meant to deal unfairly with me; so I went to work to show him that he misunderstood the whole scope of my speech, and that I really never intended to set the people at war with one another.

— First Debate with Stephen A. Douglas at Ottawa, Illinois, August 21, 1858

———✧———

Judge Douglas is going back to the era of our Revolution, and to the extent of his ability, muzzling the cannon which thunders its annual joyous return. When he invites any people willing to have slavery, to establish it, he is blowing out the moral lights around us. When he says he "cares not whether slavery is voted down or voted up."—that it is a sacred right of self government—he is in my judgment penetrating the human soul and eradicating the light of reason and the love of liberty in this American people.

— First Debate with Stephen A. Douglas at Ottawa,
Illinois, August 21, 1858

Now what is Judge Douglas' Popular Sovereignty? It is, as a principle, no other than that, if one man chooses to make a slave of another man, neither that other man nor anybody else has a right to object.

— Speech at Columbus, Ohio, September 16, 1859

I will say then that I am not, nor ever have been in favor of bringing about in any way the social and political equality of the white and black races,—that I am not nor ever have been in favor of making voters or jurors of negroes, nor of qualifying them to hold office, nor to intermarry with white people; and I will say in addition to this that there is a physical difference between the white and black races which I believe will forever forbid the two races living together on terms of social and political equality. And inasmuch as they cannot so live, while they do remain together there must be the position of superior and inferior, and I as much as any other man am in favor of having the superior position assigned to the white race. I say upon this occasion I do not perceive that because the white man is to have the superior position the negro should be denied everything. I do not understand that because I do not want a negro woman for a slave I must necessarily want her for a wife. My understanding is that I can just let her alone. . . .

> — Fourth Debate with Stephen A. Douglas at Charleston, Illinois, September 18, 1858, in response to Douglas's persistent charges that Lincoln sought social and political equality between black and white people

I was aware, when it was first agreed that Judge Douglas and I were to have these seven joint discussions, that they were the successive acts of a drama—perhaps I should say, to be enacted not merely in the face of audiences like this, but in the face of the nation. . . .

— Sixth Debate with Stephen A. Douglas at Quincy,
Illinois, October 13, 1858

In resisting the spread of slavery to new territory, and with that, what appears to me to be a tendency to subvert the first principle of free government itself my whole effort has consisted. To the best of my judgment I have labored *for*, and not *against* the Union. As I have not felt, so I have not expressed any harsh sentiment towards our Southern brethren. I have constantly declared, as I really believed, the only difference between them and us, is the difference of circumstances. . . . I have said that in some respects the contest has been painful to me. Myself, and those with whom I act have been constantly accused of a purpose to destroy the union, and bespattered with every imaginable odious epithet; and some who were friends, as it were but yesterday have made themselves most active in this. I have cultivated patience, and made no attempt at a retort.

— Last speech of Lincoln's 1858 senatorial campaign,
Springfield, Illinois, October 30, 1858

Slavery is doomed, and that within a few years. Even Judge Douglas admits it to be an evil, and an evil can't stand discussion. In discussing it we have taught a great many thousands of people to hate it who had never given it a thought before. What kills the skunk is the publicity it gives itself. What a skunk wants to do is to keep snug under the barn—in the day-time, when men are around with shot-guns.

> — Remark to David R. Locke, 1859, from *Reminiscences of Abraham Lincoln by Distinguished Men of His Time* edited by Allen Thorndike Rice

We know, Southern men declare that their slaves are better off than hired laborers amongst us. How little they *know*, whereof they *speak!* There is no permanent class of hired laborers amongst us. . . . Free labor has the inspiration of hope; pure slavery has no hope.

> — Fragment on Free Labor, September 17, 1859

We believe that the spreading out and perpetuity of the institution of slavery impairs the general welfare. We believe—nay, we know, that that is the only thing that has ever threatened the perpetuity of the Union itself.

— Speech at Cincinnati, Ohio, September 17, 1859

Wrong as we think slavery is, we can yet afford to let it alone where it is, because that much is due to the necessity arising from its actual presence in the nation; but can we, while our votes will prevent it, allow it to spread into the National Territories, and to overrun us here in these Free States? If our sense of duty forbids this, then let us stand by our duty, fearlessly and effectively.

— Speech at Cooper Union, New York City, February 27, 1860

Let us have faith that right makes might, and in that faith, let us, to the end, dare to do our duty as we understand it.

— Speech at Cooper Union, New York City, February 27, 1860

I am naturally anti-slavery. If slavery is not wrong, nothing is wrong. I can not remember when I did not so think, and feel. And yet I have never understood that the Presidency conferred upon me an unrestricted right to act officially upon this judgment and feeling.

— Letter to Albert Hodges, April 4, 1864

Whenever I hear any one arguing for slavery I feel a strong impulse to see it tried on him personally.

— Speech to 140th Indiana Regiment, March 17, 1865

We all declare for liberty; but in using the same word we do not all mean the same thing. With some the word liberty may mean for each man to do as he pleases with himself, and the product of his labor; while with others, the same word may mean for some men to do as they please with other men, and the product of other men's labor. Here are two, not only different, but incompatible things, called by the same name—liberty. And it follows that each of the things is, by the respective parties, called by two different and incompatible names—liberty and tyranny.

— Address at Sanitary Fair, Baltimore, Maryland, April 18, 1864

In giving freedom to the slave, we assure freedom to the free—honorable alike in what we give, and what we preserve. We shall nobly save, or meanly lose, the last best hope of earth. Other means may succeed; this could not fail. The way is plain, peaceful, generous, just—a way which, if followed, the world will forever applaud, and God must forever bless.

— Message to Congress, December 1, 1862

But it is dreaded that the freed people will swarm forth, and cover the whole land? Are they not already in the land? Will liberation make them any more numerous? Equally distributed among the whites of the whole country, and there would be but one colored to seven whites. Could the one, in any way, greatly disturb the seven? There are many communities now, having more than one free colored person, to seven whites; and this, without any apparent consciousness of evil from it.

— Message to Congress, December 1, 1862

– The Presidency –

The Presidency, even to the most experienced politicians, is no bed of roses; and Gen. Taylor like others, found thorns within it. No human being can fill that station and escape censure.

> — Lincoln's Eulogy on Zachary Taylor at Chicago,
> Illinois, July 25, 1850

My Dear Sir:
. . . I must in candor say I do not think myself fit for the presidency. I certainly am flattered and gratified that some partial friends think of me in that connection; but I really think it best for our cause that no concerted effort, such as you suggest, should be made. Let this be considered confidential.

> — Lincoln's letter to editor of a Rock Island newspaper
> who wished to endorse Lincoln as a presidential
> candidate, April 16, 1859

My name is new in the field; and I suppose I am not the *first* choice of a very great many. Our policy, then, is to give no offence to others—leave them in a mood to come to us, if they shall be compelled to give up their first love. This, too, is dealing justly with all, and leaving us in a mood to support heartily whoever shall be nominated. I believe I have once before told you that I especially wish to do no ungenerous things towards Governor Chase, because he gave us his sympathy in 1858, when scarcely any other distinguished man did. Whatever you may do for me, consistently with these suggestions, will be appreciated, and gratefully remembered.

> — Letter to Samuel Galloway, Ohio Republican leader
> and Lincoln supporter, on Lincoln's strategy to win the
> Republican presidential nomination, March 24, 1860

As you request, I will be entirely frank. The taste *is* in my mouth a little; and this, no doubt, disqualifies me, to some extent, to form correct opinions. You may confidently rely, however, that by no advice or consent of mine, shall my pretentions be pressed to the point of endangering our common cause.

> — Letter to Lymon Trumbull, Republican senator, on
> Lincoln's presidential aspirations, April 29, 1860

My dear Sir:

Your very kind letter of the 15th is received. Messrs. Follett, Foster & Co's Life of me is *not* by my authority; and I have scarcely been so much astounded by anything, as by their public announcement that it is authorized by me. They have fallen into some strange misunderstanding. I certainly knew they contemplated publishing a biography, and I certainly did not object to their doing so, *upon their own responsibility*. I even took pains to facilitate them. But, at the same time, I made myself tiresome, if not hoarse, with repeating to Mr. Howard, their only agent seen by me, my protest that I *authorized nothing*—would be *responsible for nothing*. How, they could so misunderstand me, passes comprehension. As a matter, *wholly my own*, I would authorize no biography, without *time*, and *opportunity* to carefully examine and consider every word of it; and, in this case, in the nature of things, I can have no such time and opportunity.

> — Letter to Samuel Galloway in response to an
> unauthorized biography of Lincoln, June 19, 1860

Give our clients to understand that the election of a President makes no change in the firm of Lincoln and Herndon. If I live I'm coming back some time, and then we'll go right on practising law as if nothing had ever happened.

> — Lincoln's remark to William H. Herndon as he left
> their law office for the last time, February 10, 1861,
> from *Herndon's Lincoln: The True Story of a Great Life* by
> William H. Herndon and Jesse W. Weik

My Friends:

No one, not in my situation, can appreciate my feeling of sadness at this parting. To this place, and the kindness of these people, I owe every thing. Here I have lived a quarter of a century, and have passed from a young to an old man. Here my children have been born, and one is buried. I now leave, not knowing when, or whether ever, I may return, with a task before me greater than that which rested upon Washington. Without the assistance of that Divine Being, who ever attended him, I cannot succeed. With that assistance, I cannot fail. Trusting in Him, who can go with me, and remain with you and be every where for good, let us confidently hope that all will yet be well. To His care commending you, as I hope in your prayers you will commend me, I bid you an affectionate farewell.

> — Lincoln's Farewell Address at Springfield, Illinois, as he
> boarded the train for Washington, February 11, 1861

We are not enemies, but friends. We must not be enemies. Though passion may have strained, it must not break our bonds of affection. The mystic chords of memory, stretching from every battle-field and patriot grave, to every heart and hearthstone, all over this broad land, will yet swell the chorus of the Union, when again touched, as surely they will be, by the better angels of our nature.

— First Inaugural Address, March 4, 1861

I am, as you know, only the servant of the people.

— Letter to James Gilmore, March 13, 1861

Dear Sir
The bearer (William) is a servant who has been with me for some time & in whom I have confidence as to his integrity and faithfulness. He wishes to enter your service. The difference of color between him & the other servants is the cause of our separation. If you can give him employment you will confer a favour on Yours truly

— Letter to Gideon Welles, March 16, 1861

I feel like the man who was tarred and feathered and ridden out of town on a rail. To the man who asked how he liked it he said: 'If it wasn't for the honour of the thing. I'd rather walk.'

> — Lincoln's response to a friend who asked him how he liked being President shortly after the inauguration, from *Lincoln Talks: A Biography in Anecdote* edited by Emanuel Hertz

My dear Sir:
On reflection I think it will not do, as a rule, for the adjutant-general to attend me wherever I go: not that I have any objection to his presence, but that it would be an uncompensating encumbrance both to him and me. When it shall occur to me to go anywhere, I wish to be free to go at once, and not to have to notify the adjutant-general and wait till he can get ready. It is better, too, for the public service that he shall give his time to the business of his office, and not to personal attendance on me. While I thank you for the kindness of the suggestion, my view of the matter is as I have stated.

> — Letter to Edwin M. Stanton regarding precautions advised for the President's safety, January 22, 1862

I claim not to have controlled events, but confess plainly that events have controlled me.

— Letter to A. G. Hodges, April 4, 1864

❧

I suppose it is good for the body. But the tired part of me is *inside* and out of reach.

— Remark made during his presidency in response to a friend's suggestion that he rest, from *The American Political Tradition: And the Men Who Made It* by Richard Hofstadter

❧

You have little idea of the terrible weight of care and sense of responsibility of this office of mine. Schenck, if to be at the head of Hell is as hard as what I have to undergo here, I could find it in my heart to pity Satan himself.

— Remark to General Robert E. Schenck, from *Reminiscences of Abraham Lincoln* edited by Allen T. Rich

❧

I have not permitted myself, gentlemen, to conclude that I am the best man in the country; but I am reminded, in this connection, of a story of an old Dutch farmer who remarked to a companion once that 'it was not best to swap horses while crossing streams.'

— Reply to Delegation from the National Union League, June 9, 1864

I desire so to conduct the affairs of this administration that if at the end, when I come to lay down the reins of power, I have lost every other friend on earth, I shall at least have one friend left, and that friend shall be down inside me.

— Reply to the Missouri Committee of Seventy, September 30, 1864

If I were to try to read, much less answer, all the attacks made on me, this shop might as well be closed for any other business. I do the very best I know how—the very best I can; and I mean to keep doing so until the end. If the end brings me out all right, what is said against me won't amount to anything. If the end brings me out wrong, ten angels swearing I was right would make no difference.

— Remark to an officer, from *Six Months at the White House with Abraham Lincoln* by F. B. Carpenter

For myself, I feel—though the tax on my time is heavy—that no hours of my day are better employed than those which thus bring me again within the direct contact and atmosphere of the average of our whole people. Men moving only in an official circle are apt to become merely official—not to say arbitrary—in their ideas, and are apter and apter, with each passing day, to forget that they only hold power in a representative capacity. Now this is all wrong. I go into these promiscuous receptions of all who claim to have business with me twice each week, and every applicant for audience has to take his turn, as if waiting to be shaved in a barber's shop. Many of the matters brought to my notice are utterly frivolous; but others are of more or less importance, and all serve to renew in me a clearer and more vivid image of that great popular assemblage out of which I sprung, and to which at the end of two years I must return.

— Remark to Colonel Charles G. Halpine, from *Six Months at the White House with Abraham Lincoln* by F. B. Carpenter

---

This morning, as for some days past, it seems exceedingly probable that this Administration will not be re-elected. Then it will be my duty to so co-operate with the President elect, as to save the Union between the election and the inauguration; as he will have secured his election on such ground that he can not possibly save it afterwards.

— Memorandum on Probable Failure of Re-election, August 23, 1864

But the rebellion continues; and now that the election is over, may not all, having a common interest, re-unite in a common effort, to save our common country? For my own part I have striven, and shall strive to avoid placing any obstacle in the way. So long as I have been here I have not willingly planted a thorn in any man's bosom. While I am deeply sensible to the high compliment of a re-election; and duly grateful, as I trust, to Almighty God for having directed my countrymen to a right conclusion, as I think, for their own good, it adds nothing to my satisfaction that any other man may be disappointed or pained by the result.

— Response to Serenade, Washington, D.C.,
November 10, 1864

Fellow-Countrymen:
At this second appearing to take the oath of the presidential office, there is less occasion for an extended address than there was at the first. Then a statement, somewhat in detail, of a course to be pursued, seemed fitting and proper. Now, at the expiration of four years, during which public declarations have been constantly called forth on every point and phase of the great contest which still absorbs the attention and engrosses the energies of the nation, little that is new could be presented. The progress of our arms, upon which all else chiefly depends, is as well known to the public as to myself; and it is, I trust, reasonably satisfactory and encouraging to all. With high hope for the future, no prediction in regard to it is ventured.

On the occasion corresponding to this four years ago, all thoughts were anxiously directed to an impending civil war. All dreaded it—all sought to avert it. While the inaugural address was being delivered from this place, devoted altogether to saving the Union without war, insurgent agents were in the city seeking to destroy it without war—seeking to dissolve the Union, and divide effects, by negotiation. Both parties deprecated war; but one of them would make war rather than let the nation survive; and the other would accept war rather than let it perish. And the war came.

One-eighth of the whole population were colored slaves, not distributed generally over the Union, but localized in the Southern part of it. These slaves constituted a peculiar and powerful interest. All knew that this interest was, somehow, the cause of the war. To strengthen, perpetuate, and extend this interest was the object for which the insurgents would rend the Union, even by war; while the government claimed no right to do more than to restrict the territorial enlargement of it.

Neither party expected for the war the magnitude or the duration which it has already attained. Neither anticipated that the cause of the conflict might cease with, or even before, the conflict itself should cease. Each looked for an easier triumph, and a result less fundamental and astounding. Both read the same Bible, and pray to the same God; and each invokes His aid against the other. It may seem strange that any men should dare to ask a just God's assistance in wringing their bread from the sweat of other men's faces; but let us judge not, that we be not judged. The prayers of both could not be answered—that of neither has been answered fully.

The Almighty has His own purposes. "Woe unto the world because of offences! for it must needs be that offences come; but woe to that man by whom the offence cometh." If we shall suppose that American slavery is one of those offences which, in the providence of God, must needs come, but which, having continued through His appointed time, He now wills to remove, and that He gives to both North and South this terrible war, as the woe due to those by whom the offence came, shall we discern therein any departure from those divine attributes which the believers in a living God always ascribe to him? Fondly do we hope—fervently do we pray—that this mighty scourge of war may speedily pass away. Yet, if God wills that it continue until all the wealth piled by the bondman's two hundred and fifty years of unrequited toil shall be sunk, and until every drop of blood drawn with the lash shall be paid by another drawn with the sword, as was said three thousand years ago, so still it must be said, "The judgments of the Lord are true and righteous altogether."

With malice toward none; with charity for all; with firmness in the right, as God gives us to see the right, let us strive on to finish the work we are in; to bind up the nation's wounds; to care for him who shall have borne the battle, and for his widow, and his orphan—to do all which may achieve and cherish a just and lasting peace among ourselves, and with all nations.

— Second Inaugural Address, March 4, 1865

Every one likes a compliment. Thank you for yours on my little notification speech, and on the recent [Second] Inaugural Address. I expect the latter to wear as well as—perhaps better than—any thing I have produced; but I believe it is not immediately popular. Men are not flattered by being shown that there has been a difference of purpose between the Almighty and them. To deny it, however, in this case, is to deny that there is a God governing the world.

— Letter to Thurlow Weed, March 15, 1865

— The Civil War —

Let there be no compromise on the question of *extending* slavery. If there be, all our labor is lost, and, ere long, must be done again. The dangerous ground—that into which some of our friends have a hankering to run—is Pop. Sov. Have none of it. Stand firm. The tug has to come, & better now, than any time hereafter.

> — Letter to Lymon Trumbull in response to news that some Republican senators were considering a compromise on the issue of slavery extension, December 10, 1860

Do the people of the South really entertain fears that a Republican administration would, *directly*, or *indirectly*, interfere with their slaves, or with them, about their slaves? If they do, I wish to assure you, as once a friend, and still, I hope, not an enemy, that there is no cause for such fears. The South would be in no more danger in this respect, than it was in the days of Washington. I suppose, however, this does not meet the case. You think slavery is *right* and ought to be extended; while we think it is *wrong* and ought to be restricted. That I suppose is the rub. It certainly is the only substantial difference between us.

— Letter to Alexander H. Stephens, the future
Confederate vice-president, written immediately after
South Carolina seceded, December 22, 1860

I say now, however, as I have all the while said, that on the territorial question—that is, the question of extending slavery under the national auspices,—I am inflexible. I am for no compromise which *assists* or *permits* the extension of the institution on soil owned by the nation.

— Letter to William H. Seward, February 1, 1861

The man does not live who is more devoted to peace than I am. None who would do more to preserve it.

— Address to the New Jersey General Assembly, Trenton,
New Jersey, February 21, 1861

Apprehension seems to exist among the people of the Southern States, that by the accession of a Republican Administration, their property, and their peace, and personal security, are to be endangered. There has never been any reasonable cause for such apprehension. Indeed, the most ample evidence to the contrary has all the while existed, and been open to their inspection. It is found in nearly all the published speeches of him who now addresses you. I do but quote from one of those speeches when I declare that "I have no purpose, directly or indirectly, to interfere with the institution of slavery in the States where it exists. I believe I have no lawful right to do so, and I have no inclination to do so." Those who nominated and elected me did so with full knowledge that I had made this, and many similar declarations, and had never recanted them.

— First Inaugural Address, March 4, 1861

In *your* hands, my dissatisfied fellow countrymen, and not in *mine*, is the momentous issue of civil war. The government will not assail *you*. You can have no conflict, without being yourselves the aggressors. *You* have no oath registered in Heaven to destroy the government, while *I* shall have the most solemn one to "preserve, protect, and defend it."

— First Inaugural Address, March 4, 1861

I think the necessity of being *ready* increases. Look to it.

> — Letter to Pennsylvania Governor Andrew G. Curtin, four
> days prior to the firing on Fort Sumter, April 8, 1861

I have desired as sincerely as any man—I sometimes think more than any other man—that our present difficulties might be settled without the shedding of blood.

> — Address to the Frontier Guard, April 26, 1861

Our popular government has often been called an experiment. Two points in it, our people have already settled—the successful *establishing*, and the successful *administering* of it. One still remains—its successful *maintenance* against a formidable internal attempt to overthrow it. It is now for them to demonstrate to the world, that those who can fairly carry an election, can also suppress a rebellion—that ballots are the rightful, and peaceful, successors of bullets; and that when ballots have fairly, and constitutionally, decided, there can be no successful appeal, back to bullets; that there can be no successful appeal, except to ballots themselves, at succeeding elections. Such will be a great lesson of peace; teaching men that what they cannot take by an election, neither can they take it by a war—teaching all, the folly of being the beginners of a war.

> — Special Message to Congress, July 4, 1861

Great honor is due to those officers who remain true, despite the example of their treacherous associates; but the greatest honor, and most important fact of all, is the unanimous firmness of the common soldiers, and common sailors. To the last man, so far as known, they have successfully resisted the traitorous efforts of those, whose commands, but an hour before, they obeyed as absolute law. This is the patriotic instinct of the plain people. They understand, without an argument, that destroying the government, which was made by Washington, means no good to them.

— Special Message to Congress, July 4, 1861

And having thus chosen our course, without guile, and with pure purpose, let us renew our trust in God, and go forward without fear, and with manly hearts.

— Special Message to Congress, July 4, 1861

The struggle of today is not altogether for today—it is for a vast future also. With a reliance on Providence, all the more firm and earnest, let us proceed in the great task which events have devolved upon us.

— First Annual Message to Congress, December 3, 1861

My dear Sir:

I have been, and am sincerely your friend; and if, as such, I dare to make a suggestion, I would say you are adopting the best possible way to ruin yourself. "Act well your part, there all the honor lies." He who does *something* at the head of one Regiment, will eclipse him who does *nothing* at the head of a hundred.

> — Letter to General David Hunter, written in response to Hunter's complaints about his appointment, December 31, 1861

My dear Sir:

Your dispatches complaining that you are not properly sustained, while they do not offend me, do pain me very much. . . . I suppose the whole force which has gone forward for you, is with you by this time; and if so, I think it is the precise time for you to strike a blow. By delay the enemy will relatively gain upon you—that is, he will gain faster, by *fortifications* and *re-inforcements*, than you can by re-inforcements alone. And, once more let me tell you, it is indispensable to *you* that you strike a blow. *I* am powerless to help this. You will do me the justice to remember I always insisted, that going down the Bay in search of a field, instead of fighting at or near Manassas, was only shifting, and not surmounting, a difficulty—that we would find the same enemy, and the same, or equal, intrenchments, at either place. The country will not fail to note—is now noting—that the present hesitation to move upon an intrenched enemy, is but the story of Manassas repeated. I beg to assure you that I have never written you, or spoken to you, in greater kindness of feeling than now, nor with a fuller purpose to sustain you, so far as in my most anxious judgment, I consistently can. *But you must act.*

> — Letter to General George B. McClellan, April 9, 1862

I expect to maintain this contest until successful, or till I die, or am conquered, or my term expires, or Congress or the country forsakes me; and I would publicly appeal to the country for this new force, were it not that I fear a general panic and stampede would follow—so hard is it to have a thing understood as it really is. I think the new force should be all, or nearly all infantry, principally because such can be raised most cheaply and quickly.

> — Letter to William H. Seward, June 28, 1862. Within days of this letter, Lincoln called for an additional 300,000 men.

The people of Louisiana—all intelligent people everywhere—know full well that I never had a wish to touch the foundations of their society, or any right of theirs. With perfect knowledge of this they forced a necessity upon me to send armies among them, and it is their own fault, not mine, that they are annoyed by the presence of General Phelps. They also know the remedy—know how to be cured of General Phelps. Remove the necessity of his presence. . . . They very well know the way to avert all this is simply to take their place in the Union upon the old terms. . . . I am a patient man—always willing to forgive on the Christian terms of repentance, and also to give ample time for repentance. Still, I must save this government, if possible. What I cannot do, of course I will not do; but it may as well be understood, once for all, that I shall not surrender this game leaving any available card unplayed.

> — Letter to Reverdy Johnson, a Baltimore Unionist who had exasperated Lincoln with his complaints about the presence of the Union forces in Louisiana, July 26, 1862

So you're the little woman who wrote the book that made this great war.

> — Remark to Harriet Beecher Stowe on her visit to the White House, November 1862, from *Abraham Lincoln: The Prairie Years and The War Years* by Carl Sandburg

Your dispatch saying "I cant get those regts. off [to Washington] because I cant get quick work out of the U.S. disbursing officer & the Paymaster" is received. Please say to these gentlemen that if they do not work quickly I will make quick work with them. . . .

> — Telegram to Massachusetts Governor John A. Andrew
> following the defeat of Union forces in Virginia, when
> Washington was under threat of attack, August 12, 1862

The will of God prevails. In great contests each party claims to act in accordance with the will of God. Both *may* be, and one *must* be, wrong. God cannot be *for* and *against* the same thing at the same time. In the present civil war it is quite possible that God's purpose is something different from the purpose of either party—and yet the human instrumentalities, working just as they do, are of the best adaptation to effect His purpose. I am almost ready to say this is probably true—that God wills this contest, and wills that it shall not end yet. By His mere quiet power, on the minds of the now contestants, He could have either *saved* or *destroyed* the Union without a human contest. Yet the contest began. And having begun He could give the final victory to either side any day. Yet the contest proceeds.

> — Meditation on the divine will, probably written
> following the Union defeat at the Second Battle of
> Bull Run, September 1862

I have just read your dispatch about sore-tongued and fatigued horses. Will you pardon me for asking what the horses of your army have done since the battle of Antietam that fatigue anything?

— Telegram to General George B. McClellan, expressing
Lincoln's frustration with McClellan's hesitation to
pursue the enemy, October 24, 1862

If I had had my way, this war would never have been commenced; If I had been allowed my way this war would have ended before this, but we find it still continues; and we must believe that He permits it for some wise purpose of His own, mysterious and unknown to us; and though with our limited understandings we may not be able to comprehend it, yet we cannot but believe, that He who made the world still governs it.

— Reply to Eliza P. Gurney and Deputation from Society
of Friends, September 28, 1862

Dear Fanny:
It is with deep grief that I learn of the death of your kind and brave Father; and, especially, that it is affecting your young heart beyond what is common in such cases. In this sad world of ours, sorrow comes to all; and, to the young, it comes with bitterest

agony, because it takes them unawares. The older have learned to ever expect it. I am anxious to afford some alleviation of your present distress. Perfect relief is not possible, except with time. You can not now realize that you will ever feel better. Is not this so? And yet it is a mistake. You are sure to be happy again. To know this, which is certainly true, will make you some less miserable now. I have had experience enough to know what I say; and you need only to believe it, to feel better at once. The memory of your dear Father, instead of an agony, will yet be a sad sweet feeling in your heart, of a purer, and holier sort than you have known before. Please present my kind regards to your afflicted mother. Your sincere friend

> — Letter to Fanny McCullough upon the death of her
> father, Lieutenant-Colonel William McCullough, who
> was a good friend of Lincoln's, December 23, 1862

Fellow citizens, we cannot escape history. We, of this Congress and this administration, will be remembered in spite of ourselves. No personal significance, or insignificance, can spare one or another of us. The fiery trial, through which we pass, will light us down in honor or dishonor, to the latest generation.

> — Second Annual Message to Congress, December 1, 1862

I have got you together to hear what I have written down. I do not wish your advice about the main matter—for that I have determined for myself.

> — Lincoln's remark at Cabinet meeting in announcing his decision to issue the Emancipation Proclamation, June 1863, from *The Living Presidency: The Resources and Dilemmas of the American Presidential Office* by Emmet John Hughes

And by virtue of the power, and for the purpose aforesaid, I do order and declare that all persons held as slaves within said designated States, and parts of States, are, and henceforward shall be free; and that the Executive government of the United States, including the military and naval authorities thereof, will recognize and maintain the freedom of said persons.

And I hereby enjoin upon the people so declared to be free to abstain from all violence, unless in necessary self-defence; and I recommend to them that, in all cases when allowed, they labor faithfully for reasonable wages.

And I further declare and make known, that such persons of suitable condition, will be received into the armed service of the United States to garrison forts, positions, stations, and other places, and to man vessels of all sorts in said service.

And upon this act, sincerely believed to be an act of justice, warranted by the Constitution, upon military necessity, I invoke the considerate judgment of mankind, and the gracious favor of Almighty God.

> — from The Emancipation Proclamation, January 1, 1863

The South had fair warning, that if they did not return to their duty, I should strike at this pillar of their strength. The promise must now be kept, and I shall never recall one word.

> — Remark to Schuyler Colfax, January 1, 1863 as quoted in
> *Six Months at the White House with Abraham Lincoln* by
> F. B. Carpenter

My dear Sir:
Your interesting communication by the hand of Major Scates is received. I never did ask more, nor ever was willing to accept less, than for all the states, and the people thereof, to take and hold their places, and their rights, in the Union, under the Constitution of the United States. For this alone have I felt authorized to struggle; and I seek neither more nor less now. Still, to use a coarse, but an expressive figure, broken eggs cannot be mended. I have issued the Emancipation Proclamation, and I cannot retract it.

> — Letter to General John A. McClernand, in response to
> intelligence that high-ranking Confederates desired
> peace and a unified nation without the Emancipation
> Proclamation, January 8, 1863

I have heard, in such way as to believe it, of your recently saying that both the Army and the Government needed a Dictator. Of course it was not *for* this, but in spite of it, that I have given you the command. Only those generals who gain successes, can set up dictators. What I now ask of you is military success, and I will risk the dictatorship. . . . And now, beware of rashness. Beware of rashness, but with energy, and sleepless vigilance, go forward, and give us victories.

— Letter to General Joseph Hooker, January 26, 1863

The colored population is the great *available* and yet *unavailed* of, force for restoring the Union.

— Letter to Andrew Johnson, March 26, 1863

And then, there will be some black men who can remember that, with silent tongue, and clenched teeth, and steady eye, and well-poised bayonnet, they have helped mankind on to this great consummation. . . .

— Letter to James C. Conkling, written for a Republican rally in Springfield, Illinois, August 26, 1863

Let your military measures be strong enough to repel the invader and keep the peace, and not so strong as to unnecessarily harass and persecute the people.

— Letter to General John M. Schofield, May 27, 1863

In a word, I would not take any risk of being entangled upon the river, like an ox jumped half over a fence, and liable to be torn by dogs, front and rear, without a fair chance to gore one way or kick the other.

— Letter to General Joseph Hooker, June 5, 1863

My Dear General:

I do not remember that you and I ever met personally. I write this now as a grateful acknowledgment for the almost inestimable service you have done the country. I wish to say a word further. When you first reached the vicinity of Vicksburg, I thought you should do what you finally did—march the troops across the neck, run the batteries with the transports, and thus go below; and I never had any faith, except a general hope that you knew better than I, that the Yazoo Pass expedition and the like could succeed. When you got below and took Port Gibson, Grand Gulf, and vicinity, I thought you should go down the river and join General Banks, and when you turned northward, east of the Big Black, I feared it was a mistake. I now wish to make the personal acknowledgment that you were right and I was wrong.

— Letter to General Ulysses S. Grant, July 13, 1863

Again, my dear general, I do not believe you appreciate the magnitude of the misfortune involved in Lee's escape. He was within your easy grasp, and to have closed upon him would, in connection with our other late successes, have ended the war. As it is, the war will be prolonged indefinitely.... Your golden opportunity is gone, and I am distressed immeasurably because of it.

— Letter to General George G. Meade, dated July 14, 1863, which Lincoln did not send

My dear Sir:

I desire that a renewed and vigorous effort be made to raise colored forces along the shores of the Mississippi. Please consult the General-in-Chief; and if it is perceived that any acceleration of the matter can be effected, let it be done....

— Letter to Edwin M. Stanton, July 21, 1863

My dear Sir:

A young son of the Senator Brown of Mississippi, not yet twenty, as I understand, was wounded, and made a prisoner at Gettysburg. His mother is sister of Mrs. P. R. Fendall, of this city. Mr. Fendall, on behalf of himself and family, asks that he and they may have charge of the boy, to cure him up, being responsible for his person and good behavior. Would it not be rather a grateful and graceful thing to let them have him?

— Letter to Edwin M. Stanton, July 28, 1863

You say you will not fight to free negroes. Some of them seem willing to fight for you; but no matter. Fight you, then, exclusively, to save the Union. I issued the proclamation on purpose to aid you in saving the Union. Whenever you shall have conquered all resistance to the Union, if I shall urge you to continue fighting, it will be an apt time then for you to declare you will not fight to free negroes. . . . But negroes, like other people, act upon motives. Why should they do any thing for us, if we will do nothing for them? If they stake their lives for us, they must be prompted by the strongest motive—even the promise of freedom. And the promise being made, must be kept.

— Letter to James C. Conkling, written for a Republican rally in Springfield, Illinois, August 26, 1863

Peace does not appear so distant as it did. I hope it will come soon, and come to stay; and so come as to be worth the keeping in all future time.

— Letter to James C. Conkling, written for a Republican
rally in Springfield, Illinois, August 26, 1863

———— ⋅⋅⋅⋅ ————

You have been called upon to make a terrible sacrifice for the Union, and a visit to that spot, I fear, will open your wounds afresh. But oh! my dear sir, if we had reached the end of such sacrifices, and had nothing left for us to do but to place garlands on the graves of those who have already fallen, we could give thanks even amidst our tears; but when I think of the sacrifices of life yet to be offered and the hearts and homes yet to be made desolate before this dreadful war, so wickedly forced upon us, is over, my heart is like lead within me, and I feel at times, like hiding in deep darkness.

— Reply to a man who told Lincoln that his only son was
lost at Gettysburg while Lincoln was on board the train
taking him there to deliver his address, November 18,
1863, from *Reminiscences of Abraham Lincoln by Distinguished
Men of His Time*, edited by Allen Thorndike Rice

———— ⋅⋅⋅⋅ ————

Four score and seven years ago our fathers brought forth on this continent, a new nation, conceived in Liberty, and dedicated to the proposition that all men are created equal.

Now we are engaged in a great civil war, testing whether that nation, or any nation so conceived and so dedicated, can long endure. We are met on a great battle-field of that war. We have come to dedicate a portion of that field, as a final resting place for those who here gave their lives that that nation might live. It is altogether fitting and proper that we should do this.

But, in a larger sense, we can not dedicate—we can not consecrate—we can not hallow—this ground. The brave men, living and dead, who struggled here, have consecrated it, far above our poor power to add or detract. The world will little note, nor long remember what we say here, but it can never forget what they did here. It is for us the living, rather, to be dedicated here to the unfinished work which they who fought here have thus far so nobly advanced. It is rather for us to be here dedicated to the great task remaining before us—that from these honored dead we take increased devotion to that cause for which they gave the last full measure of devotion—that we here highly resolve that these dead shall not have died in vain—that this nation, under God, shall have a new birth of freedom—and that government of the people, by the people, for the people, shall not perish from the earth.

— Gettysburg Address, November 19, 1863

It is easy to see that, under the sharp discipline of civil war, the nation is beginning a new life.

— Message to Congress, December 8, 1863

I, Abraham Lincoln, President of the United States, do proclaim, declare, and make known to all persons who have, directly or by implication, participated in the existing rebellion, except as hereinafter excepted, that a full pardon is hereby granted to them and each of them, with restoration of all rights of property, except as to slaves, and in property cases where rights of third parties shall have intervened, and upon the condition that every such person shall take and subscribe an oath, and thenceforward keep and maintain said oath inviolate; and which oath shall be registered for permanent preservation, and shall be of the tenor and effect following, to wit:

"I, _____, do solemnly swear, in presence of Almighty God, that I will henceforth faithfully support, protect and defend the Constitution of the United States, and the union of the States thereunder; and that I will, in like manner, abide by and faithfully support all acts of Congress passed during the existing rebellion with reference to slaves, so long and so far as not repealed, modified or held void by Congress, or by decision of the Supreme Court; and that I will, in like manner, abide by and faithfully support all proclamations of the President made during the existing rebellion having reference to slaves, so long and so far as not modified or declared void by decision of the Supreme Court. So help me God."

— Excerpt from Proclamation of Amnesty and
Reconstruction, December 8, 1863

The restoration of the Rebel States to the Union must rest upon the principle of civil and political equality of both races; and it must be sealed by general amnesty.

— Letter to James S. Wadsworth, January 1864

On principle I dislike an oath which requires a man to swear he *has* not done wrong. It rejects the Christian principle of forgiveness on terms of repentance. I think it is enough if the man does no wrong *hereafter*.

— Memorandum to Edwin M. Stanton, February 5, 1864

My dear Sir:

I congratulate you on having fixed your name in history as the first-freestate Governor of Louisiana. Now you are about to have a Convention which, among other things, will probably define the elective franchise. I barely suggest for your private consideration, whether some of the colored people may not be let in—as, for instance, the very intelligent, and especially those who have fought gallantly in our ranks. They would probably help, in some trying time to come, to keep the jewel of liberty within the family of freedom. But this is only a suggestion, not to the public, but to you alone.

— Letter to Michael Hahn, Governor of the new loyal government of Louisiana, March 13, 1864

I have never studied the art of paying compliments to women; but I must say that if all that has been said by orators and poets since the creation of the world in praise of women were applied to the women of America, it would not do them justice for their conduct during this war. I will close by saying, God bless the women of America!

— Remarks at closing of Sanitary Fair, Washington, D.C., March 18, 1864

I suppose you are going home to see your families and friends. For the service you have done in this great struggle in which we are engaged I present you sincere thanks for myself and the country. I almost always feel inclined, when I happen to say anything to soldiers, to impress upon them in a few brief remarks the importance of success in this contest. It is not merely for today, but for all time to come that we should perpetuate for our children's children this great and free government, which we have enjoyed all our lives. I beg you to remember this, not merely for my sake, but for yours. I happen temporarily to occupy this big White House. I am a living witness that any one of your children may look to come here as my father's child has. It is in order that each of you may have through this free government which we have enjoyed, an open field and a fair chance for your industry, enterprise and intelligence; that you may all have equal privileges in the race of life, with all its desirable human aspirations. It is for this the struggle should be maintained, that we may not lose our birthright—not only for one, but for two or three years. The nation is worth fighting for, to secure such an inestimable jewel.

— Speech to 166th Ohio Regiment, Washington, D.C.,
August 22, 1864

He is a brave, honest Presbyterian soldier. What a pity that we should have to fight such a gallant fellow! If we only had such a man to lead the armies of the North, the country would not be appalled with so many disasters.

> — Remark about Stonewall Jackson, from *Behind the Scenes, or, Thirty years a Slave, and Four Years in the White House* by Elizabeth Keckley

Well, even if true, I do not see what the Rebels would gain by killing or getting possession of me. I am but a single individual, and it would not help their cause or make the least difference in the progress of the war. Everything would go right on just the same. Soon after I was nominated at Chicago, I began to receive letters threatening my life. The first one or two made me a little uncomfortable, but I came at length to look for a regular installment of this kind of correspondence in every week's mail, and up to inauguration day I was in constant receipt of such letters. It is no uncommon thing to receive them now; but they have ceased to give me any apprehension.

> — Remark to F. B. Carpenter, from *Six Months at the White House with Abraham Lincoln* by F. B. Carpenter

I have seen your dispatch expressing your unwillingness to break your hold where you are. Neither am I willing. Hold on with a bull-dog gripe, and chew & choke, as much as possible.

— Telegram to General Ulysses S. Grant, August 17, 1864

The great thing about Grant, I take it, is his perfect coolness and persistency of purpose. I judge he is not easily excited,—which is a great element in an officer,—and he has the *grit* of a bull-dog! Once let him get his 'teeth' *in*, and nothing can shake him off.

— Remark to F. B. Carpenter, from *Six Months at the White House with Abraham Lincoln* by F. B. Carpenter

In addition to what I have said, allow me to remind you that no one, having control of the rebel armies, or, in fact, having any influence whatever in the rebellion, has offered, or intimated a willingness to, a restoration of the Union, in any event, or on any condition whatever. Let it be constantly borne in mind that no such offer has been made or intimated. Shall we be weak enough to allow the enemy to distract us with an abstract question which he himself refuses to present as a practical one? . . . If Jefferson Davis wishes, for himself, or for the benefit of his friends at the North, to know what I would do if he were to offer peace and re-union, saying nothing about slavery, let him try me.

> — Letter, dated August 17, 1864, to Charles D. Robinson, a Democratic editor in Wisconsin, in which Lincoln responds to the claim that he was prolonging the war in an effort to end slavery. Fearing the letter would cause confusion among his allies, Lincoln did not send it.

Much is being said about peace; and no man desires peace more ardently than I. Still I am yet unprepared to give up the Union for a peace which, so achieved, could not be of much duration.

> — Letter to Isaac Schermerhorn, September 12, 1864

Dear Madam:
I have been shown in the files of the War Department a statement of the Adjutant General of Massachusetts, that you are the mother of five sons who have died gloriously on the field of battle. I feel how weak and fruitless must be any words of mine which should attempt to beguile you from the grief of a loss so overwhelming. But I can not refrain from tendering to you the consolation that may be found in the thanks of the Republic they died to save. I pray that our Heavenly Father

may assuage the anguish of your bereavement, and leave you only the cherished memory of the loved and lost, and the solemn pride that must be yours, to have laid so costly a sacrifice upon the altar of freedom. Yours very sincerely and respectfully

— Letter to Mrs. Lydia Bixby, November 21, 1864, published in the *Boston Transcript*. (In reality, two and not five of Mrs. Bixby's sons had been killed in the war.)

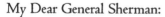

In stating a single condition of peace, I mean simply to say that the war will cease on the part of the government, whenever it shall have ceased on the part of those who began it.

— Annual Message to Congress, December 6, 1864

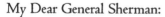

My Dear General Sherman:
Many, many thanks for your Christmas gift, the capture of Savannah. When you were about leaving Atlanta for the Atlantic coast, I was anxious, if not fearful; but feeling that you were the better judge, and remembering that "nothing risked, nothing gained," I did not interfere. Now, the undertaking being a success, the honor is all yours; for I believe none of us went further than to acquiesce. . . . But what next? I suppose it will be safe if I leave

General Grant and yourself to decide. Please make my grateful acknowledgment to your whole army—officers and men.

> — Letter to General William Tecumseh Sherman,
> December 26, 1864

Thoughtful men must feel that the fate of civilization upon this continent is involved in the issue of our contest.

> — Letter to John Maclean, December 27, 1864

Lieut. Gen. Grant:
Gen. Sheridan says "If the thing is pressed I think that Lee will surrender." Let the *thing* be pressed.

> — Telegram to General Ulysses S. Grant, April 7, 1865

— Preserving the Union —

All this talk about the dissolution of the Union is humbug—nothing but folly. *We won't* dissolve the Union, and *you shan't*.

> — Speech at Galena, Illinois, July 23, 1856, several months after joining the Republican party

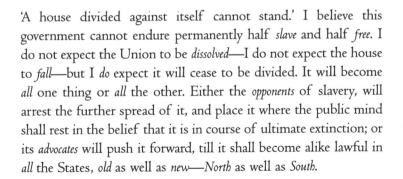

'A house divided against itself cannot stand.' I believe this government cannot endure permanently half *slave* and half *free*. I do not expect the Union to be *dissolved*—I do not expect the house to *fall*—but I *do* expect it will cease to be divided. It will become *all* one thing or *all* the other. Either the *opponents* of slavery, will arrest the further spread of it, and place it where the public mind shall rest in the belief that it is in course of ultimate extinction; or its *advocates* will push it forward, till it shall become alike lawful in *all* the States, *old* as well as *new*—*North* as well as *South*.

> — Speech at the close of the Republican state convention, Springfield, Illinois, June 16, 1858

I have often inquired of myself, what great principle or idea it was that kept this Confederacy so long together. It was not the mere matter of the separation of the colonies from the mother land; but something in that Declaration giving liberty, not alone to the people of this country, but hope to the world for all future time. It was that which gave promise that in due time the weights should be lifted from the shoulders of all men, and that *all* should have an equal chance. This is the sentiment embodied in that Declaration of Independence.

Now, my friends, can this country be saved upon that basis? If it can, I will consider myself one of the happiest men in the world if I can help to save it. If it can't be saved upon that principle, it will be truly awful. But, if this country cannot be saved without giving up that principle—I was about to say I would rather be assassinated on this spot than to surrender it.

Now, in my view of the present aspect of affairs, there is no need of bloodshed and war. There is no necessity for it. I am not in favor of such a course, and I may say in advance, there will be no blood shed unless it be forced upon the Government. The Government will not use force unless force is used against it.

— Speech at Independence Hall, Philadelphia,
Pennsylvania, February 22, 1861

Plainly, the central idea of secession, is the essence of anarchy.

— First Inaugural Address, March 4, 1861

If all do not join now to save the good old ship of the Union this voyage nobody will have a chance to pilot her on another voyage.

— Speech at Cleveland, Ohio, February 15, 1861

Physically speaking, we cannot separate. We cannot remove our respective sections from each other, nor build an impassable wall between them. A husband and wife may be divorced, and go out of the presence, and beyond the reach of each other; but the different parts of our country cannot do this. They cannot but remain face to face; and intercourse, either amicable or hostile, must continue between them. Is it possible then to make that intercourse more advantageous, or more satisfactory, *after* separation than *before*? Can aliens make treaties easier than friends can make laws? Can treaties be more faithfully enforced between aliens, than laws can among friends? Suppose you go to war, you cannot fight always; and when, after much loss on both sides, and no gain on either, you cease fighting, the identical old questions, as to terms of intercourse, are again upon you.

— First Inaugural Address, March 4, 1861

This is essentially a People's contest. On the side of the Union, it is a struggle for maintaining in the world, that form, and substance of government, whose leading object is, to elevate the condition of men—to lift artificial weights from all shoulders—to clear the paths of laudable pursuit for all—to afford all, an unfettered start, and a fair chance, in the race of life.

— Special Message to Congress, July 4, 1861

My paramount object in this struggle *is* to save the Union, and is *not* either to save or to destroy slavery. If I could save the Union without freeing *any* slave, I would do it, and if I could save it by freeing *all* the slaves, I would do it; and if I could save it by freeing some and leaving others alone, I would also do that. What I do about slavery, and the colored race, I do because I believe it helps to save the Union; and what I forbear, I forbear because I do *not* believe it would help to save the Union. I shall do *less* whenever I shall believe what I am doing hurts the cause, and I shall do *more* whenever I shall believe doing more will help the cause. . . . I have here stated my purpose according to my view of *official* duty; and I intend no modification of my oft-expressed *personal* wish that all men everywhere could be free.

— Letter to Horace Greeley, August 22, 1862

The dogmas of the quiet past are inadequate to the stormy present. The occasion is piled high with difficulty, and we must rise with the occasion. As our case is new, so we must think anew and act anew. We must disenthrall ourselves, and then we shall save our country.

— Second Annual Message to Congress, December 1, 1862

My purpose is to be, in my action, just and constitutional; and yet practical, in performing the important duty, with which I am charged, of maintaining the unity, and the free principles of our common country.

— Letter to Horatio Seymour, August 7, 1863

Was it possible to lose the nation and yet preserve the constitution? By general law life *and* limb must be protected; yet often a limb must be amputated to save a life; but a life is never wisely given to save a limb. I felt that measures, otherwise unconstitutional, might become lawful, by becoming indispensable to the preservation of the constitution, through the preservation of the nation. Right or wrong, I assumed this ground, and now avow it.

— Letter to Albert G. Hodges, April 4, 1864

– Family and Friends –

I don't know who my grandfather was; I am much more concerned to know what his grandson will be.

— from *Lincoln's Own Stories* edited by Anthony Gross

God bless my mother; all that I am or ever hope to be I owe to her.

— Remark to William H. Herndon, circa 1850, from *Herndon's Lincoln: The True Story of a Great Life* by William H. Herndon and Jesse W. Weik

I regret to learn that you have resolved to not return to Illinois. I shall be very lonesome without you. How miserably things seem to be arranged in this world. If we have no friends, we have no pleasure; and if we have them, we are sure to lose them, and be doubly pained by the loss.

— Letter to Joshua F. Speed, February 25, 1842

I reckon it will scarcely be in our power to visit Kentucky this year. Besides poverty, and the necessity of attending to business, those "coming events" I suspect would be some what in the way. I most heartily wish you and your Fanny would not fail to come. Just let us know the time a week in advance, and we will have a room provided for you at our house, and all be merry together for awhile.

— Letter to Joshua F. Speed, May 18, 1843

My Dear Father:
Your letter of the 7th was received night before last. I very cheerfully send you the twenty dollars, which sum you say is necessary to save your land from sale. It is singular that you should have forgotten a judgment against you; and it is more singular that the plaintiff should have let you forget it so long, particularly as I suppose you always had property enough to satisfy a judgment of that amount. Before you pay it, it would be well to be sure you have not paid, or at least that you cannot prove that you have paid it. Give my love to mother and all the connections.

— Letter to Thomas Lincoln, December 24, 1848

Dear Brother:

When I came into Charleston day before yesterday, I learned that you are anxious to sell the land where you live and move to Missouri. I have been thinking of this ever since, and cannot but think such a notion is utterly foolish. What can you do in Missouri better than here? Is the land any richer? Can you there, any more than here, raise corn and wheat and oats without work? Will anybody there, any more than here, do your work for you? If you intend to go to work, there is no better place than right where you are; if you do not intend to go to work, you cannot get along anywhere. Squirming and crawling about from place to place can do no good. . . . Now, do not misunderstand this letter; I do not write it in any unkindness. I write it in order, if possible, to get you to face the truth, which truth is, you are destitute because you have idled away all your time. Your thousand pretenses for not getting along better are all nonsense; they deceive nobody but yourself. Go to work is the only cure for your case.

— Lincoln's letter to his stepbrother, John D. Johnston, November 4, 1851

———⟡———

Dear Mary:

In this troublesome world, we are never quite satisfied. When you were here, I thought you hindered me some in attending to business; but now, having nothing but business—no variety—it has grown exceedingly tasteless to me. I hate to sit down and direct documents, and I hate to stay in this old room by myself. . . . And you are entirely free from head-ache? That is good—good considering it is the first spring you have been free from it since we were acquainted. I am afraid you will get so well, and fat, and young, as to be wanting to marry again. Tell Louisa I want her to watch you a little for me. Get weighed, and write me how much you weigh. I did not get rid of the impression of that foolish dream about dear Bobby till I got your letter written the same day. What did he and Eddy think of the little letters father sent them? Don't let the blessed fellows forget father. . . .

— Letter to Mary Todd Lincoln, April 16, 1848, written to her while she was visiting her family in Kentucky with their two sons

Dear Brother:
Your letter about a mail contract was received yesterday. I have made out a bid for you at $120, guaranteed it myself, got our PM here to certify it, and send it on. . . . As you make no mention of it, I suppose you had not learned that we lost our little boy. He was sick fifty-two days & died the morning of the first day of this month. It was not our *first*, but our second child. We miss him very much.

— Letter to John D. Johnston, February 23, 1850

My dear Wife:

On my return from Philadelphia, yesterday, where, in my anxiety I had been led to attend the whig convention I found your last letter. I was so tired and sleepy, having ridden all night, that I could not answer it till today; and now I have to do so in the H[ouse]. [of] R[epresentatives]. The leading matter in your letter, is your wish to return to this side of the Mountains. Will you be a good girl in all things, if I consent? Then come along, and that as soon as possible. Having got the idea in my head, I shall be impatient till I see you. . . . Come on just as soon as you can. I want to see you, and our dear— dear boys very much. Every body here wants to see our dear Bobby.

— Letter to Mary Todd Lincoln, June 12, 1848

My dear wife:

Your letter of last Sunday came last night. On that day (Sunday) I wrote the principal part of a letter to you, but did not finish it, or send it till Tuesday, when I had provided a draft for $100 which I sent in it. . . . Write me whether you got the draft, if you shall not have already done so, when this reaches you. Give my kindest regards to your uncle John, and all the family. . . . By the way, you do not intend to do without a girl, because the one you had has left you? Get another as soon as you can to take charge of the dear codgers. Father expected to see you all sooner; but let it pass; stay as long as you please, and come when you please. Kiss and love the dear rascals.

— Letter to Mary Todd Lincoln, July 2, 1848

Dear Brother:

On the day before yesterday I received a letter from Harriett, written at Greenup. She says she has just returned from your house; and that Father is very low, and will hardly recover. She also says you have written me two letters; and that although you do not expect me to come now, you wonder that I do not write. I received both your letters, and although I have not answered them, it is not because I have forgotten them, or been uninterested about them—but because it appeared to me I could write nothing which could do any good. You already know I desire that neither Father or Mother shall be in want of any comfort either in health or sickness while they live; and I feel sure you have not failed to use my name, if necessary, to procure a doctor, or any thing else for Father in his present sickness. My business is such that I could hardly leave home now, if it were not, as it is, that my own wife is sick-abed. (It is a case of baby-sickness, and I suppose is not dangerous.) I sincerely hope Father may yet recover his health. . . . Say to him that if we could meet now, it is doubtful whether it would not be more painful than pleasant; but that if it be his lot to go now, he will soon have a joyous meeting with many loved ones gone before; and where the rest of us, through the help of God, hope ere-long to join them. Write me again when you receive this.

> — Lincoln's letter to his stepbrother John D. Johnston,
> January 12, 1851. Thomas Lincoln died less than a week
> later, and Lincoln did not attend the funeral.

Dear Mother:

Chapman tells me he wants you to go and live with him. If I were you I would try it awhile. If you get tired of it (as I think you will not) you can return to your own home. Chapman feels very kindly to you; and I have no doubt he will make your situation very pleasant. Sincerely your son

> — Lincoln's letter to his stepmother after the death of his father, November 4, 1851, from *Herndon's Lincoln: The True Story of a Great Life* by William H. Herndon and Jesse W. Weik

My poor boy, he was too good for this earth. God has called him home. I know that he is much better off in heaven, but then we loved him so. It is hard, hard to have him die!

> — Spoken at Willie Lincoln's deathbed, February 20, 1862, from *Behind the Scenes, or, Thirty years a Slave, and Four Years in the White House* by Elizabeth Keckley

That blow overwhelmed me. It showed me my weakness as I had never before felt it. . . .

> — Remark to a friend from a Christian group about the death of his son Willie, from *Six Months at the White House with Abraham Lincoln* by F. B. Carpenter

Colonel, did you ever dream of a lost friend, and feel that you were holding sweet communion with that friend, and yet have a sad consciousness that it was not a reality?—just so I dream of my boy Willie.

> — Remark to army officer three months after Willie's death, from *Six Months at the White House with Abraham Lincoln* by F. B. Carpenter

It is my pleasure that my children are free and happy, and unrestrained by parental tyranny. Love is the chain whereby to bind a child to its parents.

> — Frequent remark to Mary Todd Lincoln, from *Herndon's Lincoln: The True Story of a Great Life* by William H. Herndon and Jesse W. Weik

Think you better put "Tad's" pistol away. I had an ugly dream about him.

— Telegram to Mary Todd Lincoln, June 9, 1863

—⚜—

Tell dear Tad, poor 'Nanny Goat,' is lost; and Mrs. Cuthbert & I are in distress about it. The day you left Nanny was found resting herself, and chewing her little cud, on the middle of Tad's bed. But now she's gone!

— Letter to Mary Todd Lincoln, August 8, 1863

—⚜—

My Dear Stanton:
Finding the above signature of Adams in an obscure place in the Mansion this morning and knowing of your weakness for oddities, I am sending it to you, hold on to it.—It will no doubt be much more valuable some day.

— Letter to Edwin M. Stanton, June 14, 1864

—⚜—

Lieut. General Grant:

Please read and answer this letter as though I was not President, but only a friend. My son, now in his twenty-second year, having graduated at Harvard, wishes to see something of the war before it ends. I do not wish to put him in the ranks, nor yet to give him a commission, to which those who have already served long are better entitled, and better qualified to hold. Could he, without embarrassment to you, or detriment to the service, go into your military family with some nominal rank, I, and not the public, furnishing his necessary means? If no, say so without the least hesitation, because I am as anxious, and as deeply interested, that you shall not be encumbered as you can be yourself.

> — Letter to General Ulysses S. Grant, January 19, 1865.
> Grant consented to Lincoln's request and less than a
> month later, Robert Lincoln became an assistant
> adjutant general with the rank of captain.

– Religion and the Bible –

Fellow Citizens:

A charge having got into circulation in some of the neighborhoods of this District, in substance that I am an open scoffer at Christianity, I have by the advice of some friends concluded to notice the subject in this form. That I am not a member of any Christian Church, is true; but I have never denied the truth of the Scriptures; and I have never spoken with intentional disrespect of religion in general, or of any denomination of Christians in particular. It is true that in early life I was inclined to believe in what I understand is called the "Doctrine of Necessity"—that is, that the human mind is impelled to action, or held in rest by some power, over which the mind itself has no control; and I have sometimes (with one, two or three, but never publicly) tried to maintain this opinion in argument. The habit of arguing thus however, I have, entirely left off for more than five years. And I add here, I have always understood this same opinion to be held by several of the Christian denominations. The foregoing, is the whole truth, briefly stated, in relation to myself, upon this subject. I do not think I could myself, be brought to support a man for office, whom I knew to be an open enemy of, and scoffer at, religion. Leaving the higher matter of eternal consequences, between him and his Maker, I still do not think any man has the right thus to insult the feelings, and injure the morals, of the community in which he may life. If, then, I was guilty of such conduct, I should blame no man who should condemn me for it; but I do blame those, whoever they may be, who falsely put such a charge in circulation against me.

— Handbill Addressed to the Voters of the Seventh
Congressional District, July 31, 1846, written in
response to charges from his opponent, Peter
Cartwright, a well-known Methodist preacher, that
Lincoln was an infidel. Lincoln won the election.

I know there is a God, and that He hates injustice and slavery. I see the storm coming, and I know that His hand is in it. If He has a place and work for me—and I think He has—I believe I am ready. I am nothing, but Truth is everything. I know I am right, because I know that liberty is right, for Christ teaches it, and Christ is God. I have told them that a house divided against itself cannot stand; and Christ and Reason say the same; and they will find it so.

— Remark to Newton Bateman, 1860, quoted in *Six
Months at the White House with Abraham Lincoln* by F. B.
Carpenter

When I first came to the west some forty-four or forty-five years ago, at sundown you had completed a journey of some thirty miles, which you had commenced at sunrise; and you thought you had done well. Now, only six hours have elapsed since I left my home in Illinois, where I was surrounded by a large concourse of my fellow citizens, most all of whom I could recognize; and I find myself far from home, surrounded by the thousands I now see before me, who are strangers to me. Still we are bound together, I trust, in Christianity, civilization and patriotism, and are attached to our country and our whole country. While some of us may differ in political opinions, still we are all united in one feeling for the Union.

> — Remarks at railroad station near LaFayette, Indiana a
> few hours after leaving Springfield for Washington,
> February 11, 1860, quoted by Jesse W. Weik in *The Soul
> of Abraham Lincoln* by William E. Barton

I have felt His hand upon me in great trials and submitted to His guidance, and I trust that as He shall further open the way, I will be ready to walk therein, relying on His help and trusting in His goodness and wisdom.

> — Remark to a White House visitor, June 1862, from
> *North American Review* by James F. Wilson,
> December 1896

I have often wished that I was a more devout man than I am. Nevertheless, amid the greatest difficulties of my Administration, when I could not see any other resort, I would place my whole reliance in God, knowing that all would go well, and that He would decide for the right. I thank you, gentlemen, in the name of the religious bodies which you represent, and in the name of the Common Father, for this expression of your respect. I cannot say more.

— Reply to members of the Baltimore Presbyterian Synod who came to pay their respects to Lincoln, October 1863, from *Abraham Lincoln: The Prairie Years and The War Years* by Carl Sandburg

I have never united myself to any church, because I have found difficulty in giving my assent, without mental reservation, to the long, complicated statements of Christian doctrine which characterize their Articles of Belief and Confessions of Faith. When any church will inscribe over its altar, as its sole qualification for membership, the Savior's condensed statement of the substance of both Law and Gospel, "Thou shalt love the Lord thy God with all thy heart, and with all thy soul, and with all thy mind, and thy neighbor as thyself," that church will I join with all my heart and all my soul.

— Remark to H. C. Deming, quoted in *Six Months at the White House with Abraham Lincoln* by F. B. Carpenter

Let us diligently apply the means, never doubting that a just God, in His own good time, will give us the rightful result.

— Letter to James C. Conkling, written for a Republican rally in Springfield, Illinois, August 26, 1863

I do therefore invite my fellow citizens in every part of the United States, and also those who are at sea and those who are sojourning in foreign lands, to set apart and observe the last Thursday of November next, as a day of Thanksgiving and Praise to our beneficent Father who dwelleth in the Heavens. And I recommend to them that while offering up the ascriptions justly due to Him for such singular deliverances and blessings, they do also, with humble penitence for our national perverseness and disobedience, commend to His tender care all those who have become widows, orphans, mourners or sufferers in the lamentable civil strife in which we are unavoidably engaged, and fervently implore the interposition of the Almighty Hand to heal the wounds of the nation and to restore it as soon as may be consistent with the Divine purposes to the full enjoyment of peace, harmony, tranquility and Union.

— Proclamation of Thanksgiving, October 3, 1863

I am profitably engaged in reading the Bible. Take all of this book upon reason that you can, and the balance on faith, and you will live and die a happier man.

— Remark to Joshua F. Speed, 1864, from *The Soul of Abraham Lincoln* by William E. Barton

It is a momentous thing to be the instrument, under Providence, of the liberation of a race.

— Remark to Colonel McKaye, from *Six Months at the White House with Abraham Lincoln* by F. B. Carpenter

If God now wills the removal of a great wrong, and wills also that we of the North as well as you of the South, shall pay fairly for our complicity in that wrong, impartial history will find therein new cause to attest and revere the justice and goodness of God.

— Letter to Albert Hodges, April 4, 1864

We hoped for a happy termination of this terrible war long before this; but God knows best, and has ruled otherwise. We shall yet acknowledge His wisdom and our own error therein.

— Letter to Eliza P. Gurney, September 4, 1864

In regard to this Great Book, I have but to say, it is the best gift God has given to man. All the good the Savior gave to the world was communicated through this book.

— Reply to Loyal Colored People of Baltimore upon presentation of a Bible, September 7, 1864

I have been many times driven to my knees by the overwhelming conviction that I had nowhere else to go. My own wisdom, and that of all about me, seemed insufficient for that day.

— Remark to Noah Brooks, journalist and close friend of Lincoln's, from *Lincoln Observed: The Civil War Dispatches of Noah Brooks* edited by Michael Burlingame

Don't kneel to me, that is not right. You must kneel to God only, and thank Him for the liberty you will hereafter enjoy.

> — Remark to a newly freed slave in Richmond, Virginia, April 1864, from *The Every-Day Life of Abraham Lincoln* by Francis Fisher Browne

Men are not flattered by being shown that there has been a difference of purpose between the Almighty and them. To deny it, however, in this case, is to deny that there is a God governing the world.

> — Letter to Thurlow Weed, March 15, 1865

– Intelligence and Education –

Towering genius disdains a beaten path. It seeks regions hitherto unexplored. It sees *no distinction* in adding story to story, upon the monuments of fame, erected to the memory of others. It *denies* that it is glory enough to serve under any chief. It *scorns* to tread in the footsteps of *any* predecessor, however illustrious. It thirsts and burns for distinction; and, if possible, it will have it, whether at the expense of emancipating slaves, or enslaving freemen.

— Address before the Young Men's Lyceum of
Springfield, January 27, 1838

The demon of intemperance ever seems to have delighted in sucking the blood of genius and of generosity.

— Address on Temperance, Springfield, Illinois,
February 22, 1842

I am slow to learn and slow to forget that which I have learned. My mind is like a piece of steel—very hard to scratch anything on it, and almost impossible after you get it there to rub it out.

— Remark to Joshua F. Speed, from *Herndon's Lincoln: The True Story of a Great Life* by William H. Herndon and Jesse W. Weik

To be fruitful in invention, it is indispensable to have a *habit* of observation and reflection.

— Lecture on Discoveries and Inventions, Jacksonville, Illinois, February 11, 1859

Often an idea would occur to me which seemed to have force. . . . I never let one of those ideas escape me, but wrote it on a scrap of paper and put it in that drawer. In that way I save my best thoughts on the subject, and, you know, such things often come in a kind of intuitive way more clearly than if one were to sit down and deliberately reason them out. To save the results of such mental action is true intellectual economy. . . .

— Remark to James F. Wilson, June 1862, from *Autobiography, Greatest Americans* edited by George Iles

When I read aloud two senses catch the idea: first, I see what I read; second, I hear it, and therefore I can remember it better.

— Remark to William H. Herndon about Lincoln's
constant habit of reading aloud, from *Herndon's Lincoln:
The True Story of a Great Life* by William H. Herndon
and Jesse W. Weik

—⋘⋙—

Upon the subject of education, not presuming to dictate any plan or system respecting it, I can only say that I view it as the most important subject which we as a people can be engaged in.

— Letter entitled "To the People of Sangamon County"
March 9, 1832, while a candidate for the Illinois State
Legislature

—⋘⋙—

Mr. Clay's lack of a more perfect early education, however it may be regretted generally, teaches at least one profitable lesson; it teaches that in this country, one can scarcely be so poor, but that, if he *will*, he *can* acquire sufficient education to get through the world respectably.

— Eulogy on Henry Clay, July 6, 1852

A capacity, and taste, for reading, gives access to whatever has already been discovered by others. It is the key, or one of the keys, to the already solved problems. And not only so. It gives a relish, and facility, for successfully pursuing the [yet] unsolved ones.

— Address before the Wisconsin State Agricultural
Society, Milwaukee, Wisconsin, September 30, 1859

The old general rule was that *educated* people did not perform manual labor. They managed to eat their bread, leaving the toil of producing it to the uneducated. This was not an insupportable evil to the working bees, so long as the class of drones remained very small. But *now*, especially in these free States, nearly all are educated—quite too nearly all, to leave the labor of the uneducated, in any wise adequate to the support of the whole. It follows from this that henceforth educated people must labor. Otherwise, education itself would become a positive and intolerable evil. No country can sustain, in idleness, more than a small percentage of its numbers. The great majority must labor at something productive.

— Address before the Wisconsin State Agricultural
Society, Milwaukee, Wisconsin, September 30, 1859

– Quips and Anecdotes –

If it were not for these stories, jokes, jests, I should die; they give vent—are the vents—of my moods and gloom.

> — Remark to William H. Herndon, from *The Hidden Lincoln: From the Letters and Papers of William H. Herndon* edited by Emanuel Hertz

Some of the stories are not so nice as they might be, but I tell you the truth when I say that a funny story, if it has the element of genuine wit, has the same effect on me that I suppose a good square drink of whiskey has on an old toper; it puts new life into me.

> — Remark to Illinois cavalry colonel, John F. Farnsworth, from *Abraham Lincoln: The Prairie Years and the War Years* by Carl Sandburg

I remember a good story when I hear it, but I never invented anything original. I am only a retail dealer.

> — Remark to Noah Brooks, from *Abraham Lincoln: The Prairie Years and the War Years* by Carl Sandburg

I believe I have the popular reputation of being a story-teller, but I do not deserve the name in its general sense; for it is not the story itself, but its purpose, or effect, that interests me. I often avoid a long and useless discussion by others or a laborious explanation on my own part by a short story that illustrates my point of view. So, too, the sharpness of a refusal or the edge of a rebuke may be blunted by an appropriate story, so as to save wounded feeling and yet serve the purpose. No, I am not simply a story-teller, but story-telling as an emollient saves me much friction and distress.

> — Lincoln's response to a military man's request for one of his "good stories," June 26, 1863, from "Lincoln on His Own Storytelling," by Silus W. Burt, as quoted in *Meeting Mr. Lincoln* edited by Victoria Radford

The law means nothing. I shall never marry a negress, but I have no objection to any one else doing so. If a white man wants to marry a negro woman, let him do it—*if the negro woman can stand it.*

— Remark to David R. Locke, 1859, from *Reminiscences of Abraham Lincoln by Distinguished Men of His Time* edited by Allen Thorndike Rice

———

My dear little Miss:
Your very agreeable letter of the 15th is received. I regret the necessity of saying I have no daughters. I have three sons—one seventeen, one nine, and one seven, years of age. They, with their mother, constitute my whole family. As to the whiskers, having never worn any, do you not think people would call it a piece of silly affectation if I were to begin it now? Your very sincere well-wisher

— Letter to eleven-year-old Grace Bedell of Westfield, New York, October 19, 1860. The little girl had written to Lincoln inquiring if he had a daughter and suggesting he would look better if he let his whiskers grow. Shortly thereafter, Lincoln grew a beard and upon passing through Westfield, asked to see his little admirer and told her, "You see I let these whiskers grow for you, Grace."

Give yourself no uneasiness on the subject mentioned in that of the 22nd. My note to you I certainly did not expect to see in print; yet I have not been much shocked by the newspaper comments upon it. Those comments constitute a fair specimen of what has occurred to me through life. I have endured a great deal of ridicule without much malice; and have received a great deal of kindness, not quite free from ridicule. I am used to it.

> — Letter to actor James H. Hackett, November 2, 1863,
> responding to Hackett's embarrassment for giving a
> letter that Lincoln had written him to the press

Now, my man, go away, go away! I cannot meddle in your case. I could as easily bail out the Potomac River with a teaspoon as attend to all the details of the army.

> — Remark to soldier who got in to see Lincoln at the
> White House and persisted in asking Lincoln to
> redress his grievance, from "Life in the White House
> in the Time of Abraham Lincoln" by John Hay

My dear Sir:
The lady bearer of this says she has two sons who want to work.
Set them at it if possible. Wanting to work is so rare a want that
it should be encouraged.

> — Letter to Major Ramsey, October 17, 1861

Col. Fielding:
The bearer is anxious to go to the front and die for his country.
Can't you give him a chance?

> — Note to Colonel Fielding written after Lincoln met a
> man in the street who informed him that he'd be happy
> to die for his country, if only given the chance

My dear Sir:
Hadn't we better spank this drummer boy and send him back
home to Leavenworth?

> — Letter to Edwin M. Stanton recommending leniency to a
> fourteen-year-old boy who had been court martialled and
> sentenced to be shot

Tell me what brand Grant drinks so I can send some to all my generals.

> — Remark to a congressional delegation urging that Lincoln dismiss Grant because of his drinking, 1863, from *Grant, Lincoln, and the Freedman* by Chaplain John Eaton

At another time, a gentleman addressed him, saying, "I presume, Mr. President, that you have forgotten me?" "No," was the prompt reply: "Your name is Flood. I saw you last, twelve years ago, at—" naming the place and the occasion. "I am glad to see," he continued, "that the *Flood* flows on."

> — from *Six Months at the White House with Abraham Lincoln* by F. B. Carpenter

It seems to me Mr. Capen knows nothing about the weather, in advance. He told me three days ago that it would not rain again till the 30th of April or 1st of May. It is raining now & has been for ten hours. I cannot spare any more time to Mr. Capen.

> — Memo regarding Francis L. Capen, a would-be meteorologist who had been pestering Lincoln, April 28, 1863

One night an elderly gentleman from Buffalo said, "Up our way, we believe in God and Abraham Lincoln," to which the President replied, shoving him along the line, "My friend, you are more than half right."

> — from "Life in the White House in the Time of Abraham Lincoln" by John Hay

If any personal description of me is thought desirable, it may be said, I am, in height, six feet, four inches, nearly; lean in flesh, weighing on an average one hundred and eighty pounds; dark complexion, with coarse black hair, and grey eyes—no other marks or brands recollected.

> — Autobiographical sketch, December 20, 1859

The Lord prefers common-looking people. That is the reason he makes so many of them.

> — Remark, December 23, 1863. Lincoln recalled this remark from a dream in response to someone in the crowd who recognized him and observed that he was a very common-looking man, quoted by John Hay from *Letters of John Hay and Extracts from His Diary* edited by C. L. Hay

I have stepped out upon this platform that I may see you and that you may see me, and in the arrangement I have the best of the bargain.

— Remarks at Painesville, Ohio, February 16, 1861

I presume, sir, in painting your beautiful portrait, you took your idea of me from my principles, and not from my person.

— Remark to an artist who had painted Lincoln's portrait from a photograph, from *Six Months at the White House with Abraham Lincoln* by F. B. Carpenter

For people who like that sort of thing, that is about the sort of a thing they would like.

— Remark to young poet who asked Lincoln what he thought of his newly published poems, from *Lincoln Talks: A Biography in Anecdote* edited by Emanuel Hertz

If General—had known how big a funeral he would have had, he would have died years ago.

> — Remark to David R. Locke about a recently deceased politician who was known for his great vanity, from *Lincoln Talks: A Biography in Anecdote* edited by Emanuel Hertz

Dear Sir:
Your note, requesting my "signature with a sentiment" was received, and should have been answered long since, but that it was mislaid. I am not a very sentimental man; and the best sentiment I can think of is, that if you collect the signatures of all persons who are no less distinguished than I, you will have a very undistinguishing mass of names.

> — Letter to man requesting Lincoln's autograph, January 5, 1849, from *The Wit and Wisdom of Abraham Lincoln* edited by H. Jack Lang

– Words of Wisdom –

What is to be will be and no cares of ours can arrest the decree.

> — Lincoln's often repeated "maxim and philosophy" as
> recalled by Mary Todd Lincoln, from her interview
> with William H. Herndon, September 1866, as quoted
> in *Lincoln as I Knew Him* edited by Harold Holzer

You may fool all the people some of the time; you can even fool some of the people all the time; but you can't fool all of the people all the time.

> — Remark widely attributed to Lincoln, first reported in
> *Lincoln's Yarn's & Stories* by A. McClure in 1904

Do good to those who hate you and turn their ill will to friendship.

> — frequent remark of Lincoln's recalled by Mary Todd Lincoln from her interview with William H. Herndon, September 1866, as quoted in *Lincoln as I Knew Him* edited by Harold Holzer

When the conduct of men is designed to be influenced, *persuasion,* kind, unassuming persuasion, should ever be adopted. It is an old and a true maxim, that a drop of honey catches more flies than a gallon of gall.

> — Address on Temperance, Springfield, Illinois, February 22, 1842

You are ambitious, which, within reasonable bounds, does good rather than harm.

> — Letter to General Joseph Hooker, January 26, 1863

I know not how to aid you, save in the assurance of one of mature age, and much severe experience, that you *can* not fail, if you resolutely determine, that you *will* not.

> — Letter to George C. Latham, a friend of Robert
> Lincoln's, whom Lincoln wrote to encourage when
> Latham was rejected by Harvard University,
> July 22, 1860

I believe it is an established maxim in morals that he who makes an assertion without knowing whether it is true or false, is guilty of falsehood; and the accidental truth of the assertion, does not justify or excuse him.

> — Letter to Allen N. Ford, August 11, 1846

Better give your path to a dog, than be bitten by him in contesting for the right. Even killing the dog would not cure the bite.

> — Letter to James M. Cutts, Jr., captain in Union army
> who had been court martialled for arguing with a
> fellow officer

I am rather inclined to silence, and whether that be wise or not, it is at least more unusual nowadays to find a man who can hold his tongue than to find one who cannot.

> — Remarks at the Monogahela House, February 14, 1861,
> from *The Collected Works of Abraham Lincoln* edited by Roy
> P. Basler, Volume IV

It is said an Eastern monarch once charged his wise men to invent him a sentence to be ever in view, and which should be true and appropriate in all times and situations. They presented him the words: 'And this, too, shall pass away.' How much it expresses! How chastening in the hour of pride! How consoling in the depths of affliction!

> — Address before the Wisconsin State Agricultural
> Society, Milwaukee, Wisconsin, September 30, 1859

– His Last Days –

There seemed to be deathlike stillness about me. Then I heard subdued sobs, as if a number of people were weeping. I thought I left my bed and wandered downstairs. There the silence was broken by the same pitiful sobbing, but the mourners were invisible. I went from room to room; no living person was in sight, but the same mournful sounds of distress met me as I passed along. It was light in all the rooms; every object was familiar to me, but where were all the people who were grieving as if their hearts would break? I was puzzled and alarmed. What could be the meaning of all this? Determined to find the cause of a state of things so mysterious and so shocking, I kept on until I arrived at the East Room, which I entered. Before me was a catafalque on which was a form wrapped in funeral vestments. Around it were stationed soldiers who were acting as guards; there was a throng of people, some gazing mournfully upon the catafalque, others weeping pitifully. "Who is dead in the White House?" I demanded of one of the soldiers. "The President," was the answer. "He was killed by an assassin." There came a loud burst of grief from the crowd which woke me from my dream.

> — Lincoln's recounting of dream to Mary Todd Lincoln,
> April 1865, from *Abraham Lincoln: The Prairie Years and The
> War Years* by Carl Sandburg

Fellow Citizens:

I am very greatly rejoiced to find that an occasion has occurred so pleasurable that the people cannot restrain themselves. I suppose that arrangements are being made for some sort of a formal demonstration, this, or perhaps, tomorrow night. If there should be such a demonstration, I, of course, will be called upon to respond, and I shall have nothing to say if you dribble it all out of me before. I see you have a band of music with you. I propose closing up this interview by the band performing a particular tune which I will name. Before this is done, however, I wish to mention one or two little circumstances connected with it. I have always thought 'Dixie' one of the best tunes I have ever heard. Our adversaries over the way attempted to appropriate it, but I insisted yesterday that we fairly captured it. I presented the question to the Attorney General, and he gave it as his legal opinion that it is our lawful prize. I now request the band to favor me with its performance.

— Response to Serenade, Washington, D.C., April 10, 1865

We meet this evening, not in sorrow, but in gladness of heart. The evacuation of Petersburg and Richmond, and the surrender of the principal insurgent army, give hope of a righteous and speedy peace whose joyous expression can not be restrained. In the midst of this, however, He, from Whom all blessings flow, must not be forgotten. A call for a national thanksgiving is being prepared, and will be duly promulgated. Nor must those whose harder part gives us the cause of rejoicing, be overlooked. Their honors must not be parcelled out with others. I myself, was near the front, and had the high pleasure of transmitting much of the good news to you; but no part of the honor, for plan or execution, is mine. To Gen. Grant, his skilful officers, and brave men, all belongs. The gallant Navy stood ready, but was not in reach to take active part.

By these recent successes the re-inauguration of the national authority—reconstruction—which has had a large share of thought from the first, is pressed much more closely upon our attention. It is fraught with great difficulty. Unlike the case of a war between independent nations, there is no authorized organ for us to treat with. No one man has authority to give up the rebellion for any other man. We simply must begin with, and mould from, disorganized and discordant elements. Nor is it a small additional embarrassment that we, the loyal people, differ among ourselves as to the mode, manner, and means of reconstruction. . . . We all agree that the seceded States, so called, are out of their proper practical relation with the Union; and that the sole object of the government, civil and military, in regard to those States is to again get them into that proper practical relation. I believe it is not only possible, but in fact, easier, to do this, without deciding, or even considering, whether these states have even been out of the Union, than with it. Finding themselves safely at home, it would be utterly immaterial whether they had ever been abroad. Let us all join in doing the acts necessary to restoring the proper practical relations between these states and the Union; and each forever after, innocently indulge his own opinion whether, in doing the acts, he brought the States from without, into the Union, or only gave them proper assistance, they never having been out of it.

> — Lincoln's last speech, given from a window in the
> White House to a crowd that had gathered to celebrate
> Lee's surrender, April 11, 1865

Well, my son, you have returned safely from the front. The war is now closed, and we soon will live in peace with the brave men that have been fighting against us. I trust that the era of good feeling has returned with the war, and that henceforth we shall live in peace. Now listen to me, Robert: you must lay aside your uniform, and return to college. I wish you to read law for three years, and at the end of that time I hope that we will be able to tell whether you will make a lawyer or not.

> — Remark to Robert Lincoln on the morning of April
> 14, 1865, from *Behind the Scenes, or, Thirty years a Slave, and
> Four Years in the White House* by Elizabeth Keckley

I think it providential that this great rebellion is crushed just as Congress has adjourned and there are none of the disturbing elements of that body to hinder and embarrass us. If we are wise and discreet we shall reanimate the States and get their governments in successful operation, with order prevailing and the Union reestablished before Congress comes together in December . . . I hope there will be no persecution, no bloody work after the war is over. No one need expect me to take any part in hanging or killing those men, even the worst of them. Frighten them out of the country, open the gates, let down the bars, scare them off. Enough lives have been sacrificed.

> — Lincoln's remarks in morning session with his Cabinet and Ulysses S. Grant, April 14, 1865, as recorded in the diary of Gideon Welles, from *Abraham Lincoln: The Prairie Years and The War Years* by Carl Sandburg

No, I rather think not. When you have an elephant by the hind leg, and he is trying to run away, it's best to let him run.

> — Remark to Assistant Secretary of War Charles A. Dana, April 14, 1865, about whether to arrest Jacob Thompson, a Confederate commissioner, whose planned escape that night to Liverpool was made known to the War Department, from *Abraham Lincoln: The Prairie Years and The War Years* by Carl Sandburg

At three o'clock in the afternoon, he drove out with me in the open carriage. In starting, I asked him if anyone should accompany us. He immediately replied—"No—I prefer to ride by ourselves today." During the drive he was so gay that I said to him, laughingly, "Dear Husband, you almost startle me by your great cheerfulness." He replied, "and well I may feel so, Mary; I consider *this day*, the war has come to a close" and then added, "We must *both* be more cheerful in the future—between the war and the loss of our darling Willie—we have both, been very miserable."

> — Mary Todd Lincoln's recounting of her conversation
> with Lincoln on the day of the assassination, from
> Mary Todd Lincoln's letter to F. B. Carpenter,
> November 1865, as quoted in *Lincoln as I Knew Him*
> edited by Harold Holzer

Now he belongs to the ages.

> — Spoken by Edwin M. Stanton, upon Lincoln's death at
> 7:22 a.m. on April 15, 1865

— Remembrances of
Abraham Lincoln —

Abe was about nine years of age when I landed in Indiana. The country was wild, and desolate. Abe was a good boy; he didn't like physical labor, was diligent for knowledge, wished to know, and if pains and labor would get it, he was sure to get it. He was the best boy I ever saw. He read all the books he could lay his hands on. . . . Abe, when old folks were at our house, was a silent and attentive observer, never speaking or asking questions till they were gone, and then he must understand everything, even to the smallest thing, minutely and exactly; he would then repeat it over to himself again and again, sometimes in one form and then in another, and when it was fixed in his mind to suit him, he became easy and he never lost that fact or his understanding of it.

> —Sara Bush Johnston Lincoln, Lincoln's stepmother, in a
> letter to William H. Herndon, September 8, 1865, from
> *The Hidden Lincoln: From the Letters and Papers of William H.*
> *Herndon* edited by Emanuel Hertz

His strength, kindness of manner, love of fairness and justice, his original and unique sayings, his power of mimicry, his perseverance—all made a combination rarely met with on the frontier.

> — William H. Herndon's remarks about young Abraham Lincoln, from *Herndon's Lincoln: The True Story of a Great Life* by William H. Herndon and Jesse W. Weik

---

Lincoln had the tenderest heart for any one in distress, whether man, beast, or bird. Many of the gentle and touching sympathies of his nature, which flowered so frequently and beautifully in the humble citizen at home, fruited in the sunlight of the world when he had power and place. He carried from his home on the prairies to Washington the same gentleness of disposition and kindness of heart.

> — Joshua F. Speed, from his lecture "Reminiscences of Abraham Lincoln," as quoted in *Lincoln as I Knew Him* edited by Harold Holzer

---

Mr. Lincoln was the kindest, most tenderhearted, and loving husband and father in the world. He gave us all unbounded liberty, said to me always when I asked him for anything: you know what you want—go and get it. He never asked me if it was necessary. He was very, very indulgent to his children—chided or praised for it he always said, "It is my pleasure that my children are free, happy, and unrestrained by parental tyranny. Love is the chain whereby to lock a child to its parent. . . ."

> — Mary Todd Lincoln from her interview with
> William H. Herndon, September 1866, as quoted
> in *Lincoln as I Knew Him* edited by Harold Holzer

Lincoln's favorite position when unravelling some knotty law point was to stretch both of his legs at full length upon a chair in front of him. In this position, with books on the table near by and in his lap, he worked up his case. No matter how deeply interested in his work, if any one came in he had something humorous and pleasant to say, and usually wound up by telling a joke or an anecdote. I have heard him relate the same story three times within as many hours to persons who came in at different periods, and every time he laughed as heartily and enjoyed it as if it were a new story. His humor was infectious. I had to laugh because I thought it funny that Mr. Lincoln enjoyed a story so repeatedly told.

> — William H. Herndon, in *Herndon's Lincoln: The True Story
> of a Great Life* by William H. Herndon and Jesse Weik

When Lincoln rose to speak, I was greatly disappointed. He was tall, tall—oh, how tall! and so angular and awkward that I had, for an instant, a feeling of pity for so ungainly a man. . . . But pretty soon he began to get into his subject; he straightened up, made regular and graceful gestures; his face lighted as with an inward fire; the whole man was transfigured. I forgot his clothes, his personal appearance, and his individual peculiarities. Presently, forgetting myself, I was on my feet with the rest, yelling like a wild Indian, cheering this wonderful man.

> — From a literary critic present at Lincoln's 1860 Cooper Union address in New York

In conversation, he was a patient, attentive listener, rather looking for the opinion of others, than hazarding his own, and trying to view a matter in all of its phases before coming to a conclusion.

> — William E. Doster, from *Lincoln and Episodes of the Civil War*

Mr. Lincoln, as every one knows, was far from handsome. He was not admired for his graceful figure and finely moulded face, but for the nobility of his soul and the greatness of his heart.

> — Elizabeth Keckley, from *Behind the Scenes, or, Thirty years a Slave, and Four Years in the White House* by Elizabeth Keckley

If I was asked what it was that threw such charm around him, I would say that it was his perfect naturalness. He could act no part but his own. He copied no one either in manner or style.

> — Joshua F. Speed from his lecture "Reminiscences of Abraham Lincoln" as quoted in *Lincoln as I Knew Him* edited by Harold Holzer

The President impressed me more favourably than I had hoped. A frank, sincere, well meaning man, with a lawyer's habit of mind, good clear statement of his fact, correct enough, not vulgar, as described, but with a boyish cheerfulness. . . .

> — Ralph Waldo Emerson, from his Journal

Beneath a smooth surface of candor and apparent declaration of all his thoughts and feelings, he exercised the most exalted tact and the wisest discrimination. He handled and moved men remotely as we do pieces upon a chess-board. He retained through life all the friends he ever had, and he made the wrath of his enemies to praise him. This was not by cunning or intrigue, in the low acceptance of the term, but by far-seeing reason and discernment.

> — Leonard Swett, long-time friend of Lincoln, from *Herndon's Lincoln: The True Story of a Great Man* by William H. Herndon and Jesse W. Weik

No man was ever more free from affectation, and the distaste that he felt for form, ceremony, and personal parade was genuine. Yet he was not without a certain dignity of bearing and character that commanded respect. At times, too, he rebuked those who presumed too far on his habitual good-nature and affable kindness. . . . An old acquaintance of the President, whom he had not seen for many years, visited Washington. Lincoln desired to give him a place. Thus encouraged, the visitor, who was an honest man, but wholly inexperienced in public affairs or in business, asked for a high office. The President was aghast, and said, "Good gracious! Why didn't he ask to be Secretary of the Treasury and have done with it?" Afterward, he said: "Well, now, I never thought M. had anything more than average ability, when we were young men together—and he wants to be superintendent of the mint!" He paused, and added, with a queer smile, "But then, I suppose he thought the same thing about me, and—here I am."

— Noah Brooks, from *Lincoln As I Knew Him* edited by Harold Holzer

Lincoln had the most comprehensive, the most judicious mind; he was the least faulty in his conclusions of any man I have ever known. He never stepped too soon, and he never stepped too late. . . . This unerring judgment, this patience which waited and which knew when the right time had arrived, is an intellectual quality that I do not find exercised upon any such scale and with such absolute precision by any other man in history. It proves Abraham Lincoln to have been intellectually one of the greatest of rulers. If we look through the record of great men, where is there one to be placed beside him? I do not know.

> — Charles A. Dana, Assistant Secretary of War during Lincoln's administration, from *Recollections of the Civil War with the Leaders at Washington and in the Field in the Sixties* by Ida Tarbell

---

The truth about this whole matter is that Mr. Lincoln read less and thought more than any man in his sphere in America. No man can put his finger on any great book written in the last or present century that Lincoln ever read. When he was young he read the Bible and when of age he read Shakespeare. This latter book was scarcely ever out of his mind and his hands. Mr. Lincoln is acknowledged to be a great, very great man, but the question is: What made him great? I repeat that he read less and thought more than any man, of his standing and in his own sphere, in America or probably in the world; he possessed originality and power of thought in an eminent degree; he was cautious, skeptical, cool, concentrated with continuity of reflection, was patient, persistent, and enduring. These are some of the grounds of his wonderful power and success.

> — William H. Herndon, from *The Hidden Lincoln: From the Letters and Papers of William H. Herndon* edited by Emanuel Hertz

In all my interviews with Mr. Lincoln I was impressed with his entire freedom from popular prejudice against the colored race. He was the first great man that I talked with in the United States freely, who in no single instance reminded me of the difference between himself and myself, of the difference of color, and I thought that all the more remarkable because he came from a state where there were black laws. I account partially for his kindness to me because of the similarity with which I had fought my way up, we both starting at the lowest round of the ladder. . . . Then, too, there was another feeling that I had with reference to him, and that was that while I felt I was in the presence of a very great man, as great as the greatest, I felt as though I could go and put my hand on him if I wanted to, to put my hand on his shoulder. Of course I did not do it, but I felt that I could. I felt as though I was in the presence of a big brother, and that there was safety in his atmosphere.

— Frederick Douglass, from *Reminiscences of Abraham Lincoln by Distinguished Men of His Time*, edited by Allen Thorndike Rice

---

When I entered the room, the members of the Cabinet and many distinguished officers of the army were grouped around the body of their fallen chief. They made room for me, and, approaching the body, I lifted the white cloth from the white face of the man that I had worshipped as an idol—looked upon as a demi-god.

Not-withstanding the violence of the death of the President, there was something beautiful as well as grandly solemn in the expression of the placid face. There lurked the sweetness and gentleness of childhood, and the stately grandeur of godlike intellect. I gazed long at the face, and turned away with tears in my eyes and a choking sensation in my throat. Ah! never was man so widely mourned before. The whole world bowed their heads in grief when Abraham Lincoln died.

— Elizabeth Keckley, from *Behind the Scenes, or, Thirty years a Slave, and Four Years in the White House* by Elizabeth Keckley

No one who personally knew him but will now feel that the deep, furrowed sadness of his face seemed to forecast his fate. The genial gentleness of his manner, his homely simplicity, the cheerful humor that never failed, are now seen to have been but the tender light that played around the rugged heights of his strong and noble nature. It is small consolation that he died at the moment of the war when he could best be spared, for no nation is ever ready for the loss of such a friend. But it is something to remember that he lived to see the slow day breaking. Like Moses, he had marched with us through the wilderness. From the height of patriotic vision he beheld the golden fields of the future waving in peace and plenty. He beheld, and blessed God, but was not to enter in.

— *Harper's Weekly*, April 29, 1865

And now the martyr is moving in triumphal march, mightier than when alive. The nation rises up at every stage of his coming. Cities and states are his pall-bearers, and the cannon speaks the hours with solemn progression. Dead, dead, dead, he yet speaketh. Is Washington dead? Is Hampden dead? Is any man that was ever fit to live dead? Disenthralled of flesh, risen to the unobstructed sphere where passion never comes, he begins his illimitable work. His life is now grafted upon the infinite, and will be fruitful as no earthly life can be. Pass on, thou that hast overcome. Ye people, behold the martyr whose blood, as so many articulate words, pleads for fidelity, for law, for liberty.

> — Henry Ward Beecher, "Sermon at Plymouth Church,
> Brooklyn, New York, Sunday Morning,
> April 23, 1865"

Why, if the old Greeks had had this man, what trilogies of plays—what epics—would have been made out of him! How the rhapsodes would have recited him! How quickly that quaint tall form would have enter'd into the region where men vitalize gods, and gods divinify men! But Lincoln, his times, his death—great as any, any age—belong altogether to our own.

> — Walt Whiman, "Death of Abraham Lincoln," 1879

He was not a born king of men, ruling by the restless might of his natural superiority, but a child of the people, who made himself a great persuader, therefore a leader, by dint of firm resolve, and patient effort, and dogged perseverance. He slowly won his way to eminence and renown by ever doing the work that lay next to him—doing it with all his growing might—doing it as well as he could, and learning by his failure, when failure was encountered, how to do it better.

— Horace Greeley, newspaper publisher

Of all the men I ever met, he seemed to possess more of the elements of greatness, combined with goodness, than any other.

— William T. Sherman from *Memoirs of General William T. Sherman*

Abraham Lincoln had a moral elevation most rare in a statesman, or indeed in any man.

— William Gladstone, British statesman

While it is true that the details of the private life of a public man have always a great interest in the minds of some—it is after all his works which make him live—& the rest is but secondary.

— Robert Todd Lincoln from *Herndon's Informants* edited by Douglas L. Wilson and Rodney O. Davis

Mr. Lincoln was the central figure of our age, and on him were concentrated the love, the faith, the reverence, the hate, the fear, and the calumny, of half the civilized world. The 'plain people' understood him better than did the politicians; and he in turn had a wonderful perception of the real condition of the popular heart and will.

— William O. Stoddard from *White House Sketches*

The greatness of Napoleon, Caesar or Washington is only moonlight by the sun of Lincoln. His example is universal and will last thousands of years. . . . He was bigger than his country— bigger than all the Presidents together . . . and as a great character he will live as long as the world lives.

— Leo Tolstoy, *The World*, New York, 1909

Five score years ago, a great American, in whose symbolic shadow we stand today, signed the Emancipation Proclamation. This momentous decree came as a great beacon light of hope to millions of Negro slaves who had been seared in the flames of withering injustice. It came as a joyous daybreak to end the long night of their captivity.

— Martin Luther King, Jr., "I Have a Dream," Speech at the Lincoln Memorial, August 1963

———

He no longer stands for what is best in American life and genius, but for what is best in humanity. He belongs to the world, not alone to us.

— Noah Brooks in the *New York Times*, February 12, 1898

———

– Chronology –

February 12, 1809. Abraham Lincoln is born in a one-room log cabin on Nolin Creek in Kentucky. He is the second child of Thomas Lincoln (a farmer and carpenter) and Nancy Hanks Lincoln. He has one sister, Sarah, who is two years older than him. He is named Abraham after his paternal grandfather.

1811. Thomas Lincoln moves his family several miles away from Abraham Lincoln's birthplace to a 230-acre farm on Knob Creek.

1812. A brother, Thomas, is born, and dies in infancy.

1815. Abraham and Sarah attend school in a log schoolhouse for a short time in the fall. Neither Thomas nor Nancy Hanks Lincoln can read, and Thomas can write only his name.

1816. Abraham and Sarah again attend school briefly in the fall. Thomas Lincoln, involved in a lawsuit over the title to his land, moves his family across the Ohio River to settle in the backwoods of Indiana in December.

1817. Abraham helps his father clear the land for planting. They are later joined by Nancy Hanks, Lincoln's aunt and uncle (the Sparrows), and their foster son Dennis Hanks, aged 19, who becomes Lincoln's companion.

1818. The Sparrows die of milk sickness in September and Nancy Hanks Lincoln dies of milk sickness on October 5.

1819. On December 2, Thomas Lincoln marries Sarah Bush Johnston, a 31-year-old widow with three children, Elizabeth, John, and Matilda.

1820. Abraham and Sarah attend school for a brief period.

1822. Abraham attends school for several months.

1824. Abraham helps with plowing and planting and does work-for-hire to help neighbors. He attends school in the fall and winter and reads books, including the family Bible and other books that he borrows from neighbors, whenever he can.

1827. Abraham works as a boatman and farmhand near Troy, Indiana.

1828. Abraham's sister Sarah, now married, dies in childbirth on January 20. In the spring, Abraham, aged 19, and Allen Gentry leave Indiana on a flatboat trip to New Orleans with cargo of farm produce. While trading in Louisiana, they fend off seven black men who try to rob them. In New Orleans, Lincoln witnesses a slave auction.

1830. Abraham moves with his family to Illinois where they settle on uncleared land along the Sangamon River. Abraham makes his first political speech, in favor of improving navigation on the Sangamon River.

1831. Abraham builds a flatboat with his stepbrother and cousin and makes another trip to New Orleans with produce and livestock. He returns to Illinois in the summer and moves to New Salem in Sangamon County, though his family has moved to Coles County, Illinois. He works as a store clerk and sleeps in the back of the store. He wrestles a man named Jack Armstrong to a draw, and makes friends and earns the respect of local men as a result. He learns basic mathematics, reads Shakespeare and Robert Burns and takes part in a local debating society.

1832. In March, Lincoln becomes candidate for the Illinois General Assembly. The Black Hawk War breaks out. Lincoln volunteers for Illinois militia in early April and is elected company captain. He reenlists as a private after his company is disbanded in late May and serves until July 10, though he does not see any action. Lincoln loses the election on August 6, and becomes a partner with William F. Berry in a New Salem general store.

1833. The store fails and Lincoln is left badly in debt. He begins to write deeds and mortgages for neighbors and works as a hired hand. He is appointed postmaster of New Salem in May. In the fall, he is appointed deputy surveyor of Sangamon County.

1834. On August 4, Lincoln is elected to the Illinois General Assembly for the Whig party representing Sangamon County. He begins to study law. He meets Stephen A. Douglas, a 21-year-old lawyer and Democrat who is active in politics.

1835. Ann Rutledge dies in August from fever at the age of 22. Lincoln met and became friends with Ann in 1831. The two were romantically linked and he reportedly fell into a deep depression upon her death.

1836. Lincoln wins reelection on August 1, and has become a leader of the Whig party. On September 9, he receives his license to practice law. He begins a courtship of sorts with Mary Owens, a 28-year-old Kentucky woman who was visiting her sister in New Salem. He suffers an episode of depression (which he refers to as "hypochondria") following his return in early December for new legislative session.

1837. Lincoln and others from the Whig party are successful in moving the Illinois state capital from Vandalia to Springfield. On April 15, he settles in Springfield and rooms with storeowner Joshua F. Speed, who becomes his lifelong friend. He becomes law partners with John T. Stuart and begins his practice of law in both civil and criminal areas, primarily as a defense attorney. Mary Owens rejects his proposal of marriage, and the courtship ends in August.

1838. On August 6, Lincoln is reelected to the Illinois General Assembly, and serves as Whig floor leader.

1839. Lincoln travels through nine counties in central and eastern Illinois as a lawyer on the Eighth Judicial Circuit. In December, he is admitted to practice in U.S. Circuit Court. Lincoln meets Mary Todd at a dance. She is the 21-year-old daughter of a prominent Whig banker from Kentucky.

1840. In June, Lincoln argues his first case before the Illinois Supreme Court. He will appear before the state high court a total of 240 times. On August 3, he is reelected to the legislature. He gets engaged to Mary Todd.

1841. On January 1, Lincoln breaks off his engagement to Mary Todd. He suffers severe depression for weeks and is absent from the legislature for several days. He dissolves his law partnership with John T. Stuart and forms a new partnership with Stephen T. Logan.

1842. Lincoln does not seek reelection to the legislature. He marries Mary Todd on November 4 in Springfield after having secretly resumed their courtship.

1843. Lincoln makes an unsuccessful bid for the Whig nomination for U.S. Congress. Robert Todd Lincoln is born on August 1.

1844. In May, the Lincolns move into a house in Springfield purchased for $1,500.00 which they live in until 1861. In December, Lincoln dissolves his law practice with Stephen T. Logan and sets up his own practice, taking in William H. Herndon as a junior partner.

1846. On March 10, Edward Baker Lincoln is born. Lincoln wins the congressional nomination of the Whig party on May 1. He is elected to the U.S. House of Representatives on August 3.

1847. The Lincolns move into a boarding house near the Capitol. Lincoln takes his seat in the House of Representatives on December 6.

1848. On January 22, Lincoln gives a speech opposing President Polk's war policy with regard to Mexico. He attends the national Whig convention in June supporting General Zachary Taylor as presidential nominee. Lincoln does not seek a second term in Congress.

1849. Lincoln votes to exclude slavery from federal territories and end slave trade in the District of Columbia but doesn't take part in the congressional debates on slavery. On March 7 and 8, Lincoln makes his only appearance before the U.S. Supreme Court in a case involving the Illinois statute of limitations, but is unsuccessful. He returns to Springfield on March 31 and later resumes his law practice.

1850. On February 1, son Edward dies after being ill for two months. Lincoln returns to the Eighth Judicial Circuit and gains a reputation for being an excellent lawyer. On December 21, William Wallace Lincoln is born.

1851. On January 17, Thomas Lincoln dies. Lincoln does not travel to the funeral.

1853. Thomas (Tad) Lincoln is born on April 4.

1854. Lincoln's interest in politics is re-ignited when Congress passes the Kansas-Nebraska Act on May 30, which repealed the antislavery restriction in the Missouri Compromise. Lincoln speaks against the Act at Bloomington, Springfield, and Peoria appearing either before or after Senator Stephen A. Douglas, the principal author of the Act. Lincoln is elected to the legislature, but declines, to try instead for a seat in the Senate.

1855. On February 8, Lincoln loses bid for a Senate seat.

1856. In May, Lincoln helps to establish the Republican party of Illinois. At the first Republican convention in Philadelphia in June, Lincoln gets 110 votes for the vice-presidential nomination, giving him national recognition.

1857. On June 26, Lincoln delivers major speech in Springfield against the Dred Scott decision by the Supreme Court.

1858. Lincoln accepts endorsement on June 16 by Republican state convention for Senate seat, opposing Democrat Stephen A.

Douglas. Lincoln delivers "House Divided" speech at the state convention in Springfield. Lincoln and Douglas agree to seven debates which are attended by thousands of people.

1859. On January 5, Illinois legislature reelects Douglas to the Senate over Lincoln by a vote of 54 to 46. From August through October, Lincoln makes speeches for Republican candidates in Iowa, Ohio, and Wisconsin. Lincoln's name is mentioned as a possible presidential candidate.

1860. On February 27, Lincoln delivers famous address on slavery and the founding fathers to an audience of 1,500 at Cooper Union in New York City. The Lincoln-Douglas debates are published in book form in March. On May 18, Lincoln is nominated to be the Republican candidate for President. On November 6, Lincoln is elected the 16th U.S. President and the first Republican, receiving 180 of 303 possible electoral votes and 40 percent of the popular vote. On December 20, South Carolina secedes from the Union, followed within two months by Mississippi, Florida, Alabama, Georgia, Louisiana, and Texas.

1861. February 11, Lincoln gives his farewell address to Springfield, one day before his 52nd birthday and leaves for Washington by train. He receives a warning during the trip about a possible assassination attempt. He is inaugurated on March 4. On April 12, the Civil War begins with an attack on Fort Sumter by Confederate troops. On April 15, Lincoln issues a call for 75,000 volunteers. On April 17, Virginia secedes, followed within five weeks by

North Carolina, Tennessee, and Arkansas, forming a Confederacy of eleven states. On July 21, the Union army is defeated at the Battle of Bull Run. On July 27, Lincoln appoints George B. McClellan as commander of the Department of the Potomac. On November 1, Lincoln appoints McClellan as commander of the Union army.

1862. On February 20, Willie Lincoln dies at the White House, most likely of typhoid fever. He is eleven years old. Mary Todd Lincoln is consumed with her grief and never fully recovers from the loss. On March 11, Lincoln removes McClellan as general-in-chief and takes direct control of the Union armies. On April 6, the Confederates launch a surprise attack on General Ulysses S. Grant's forces at Shiloh. There are 13,000 Union killed and wounded and 10,000 Confederates. Lincoln resists pressure to dismiss Grant, who is blamed for the heavy losses. On April 16, Lincoln signs an Act that abolishes slavery in the District of Columbia. In late August, the Union is defeated at the second Battle of Bull Run. On September 17, General Robert E. Lee's Confederate forces are halted by the Union forces under the command of General McClellan at Antietam in Maryland. With 26,000 men dead, wounded, or missing by nightfall, it remains the bloodiest day in U.S. military history. On September 22, Lincoln issues a preliminary Emancipation Proclamation freeing the slaves. On November 5, Lincoln names Ambrose E. Burnside as commander of the Army of the Potomac, replacing McClellan. On December 13, the Union suffers a crushing defeat at Fredericksburg with the loss of 12,653 men.

1863. On January 1, Lincoln issues final Emancipation Proclamation freeing all slaves in territories held by the Confederates. On January 25, Lincoln appoints Joseph Hooker as commander of the Army of the Potomac, replacing Burnside. On February 25, Lincoln approves a bill creating a national banking system and signs an act on March 3 introducing military conscription. The Union forces are defeated at the Battle of Chancellorsville on May 1–4. On June 28, Lincoln replaces Hooker with George G. Meade, during Lee's invasion of Pennsylvania. On July 1–3, the Union is victorious at Gettysburg and on July 4 at Vicksburg, which is captured by Grant and the Army of the West. On August 10, Lincoln meets with Frederick Douglass to discuss issues of recruitment and treatment of Negro troops. In September, Lincoln appoints Grant to command of all operations in the western theater. On November 19, Lincoln delivers the dedication address at the Gettysburg National Cemetery to an audience of 15,000 to 20,000. On December 8, Lincoln issues proclamation of amnesty and reconstruction to begin the process of restoring the Union.

1864. On March 12, Lincoln appoints Grant as general-in-chief of all the Federal armies while William T. Sherman succeeds Grant as commander in the Western theater. On June 8, Lincoln is nominated for re-election by the National Union Convention, which consisted of a coalition of Republicans and War Democrats. On September 2, Sherman and his army capture Atlanta. Lincoln later approves of Sherman's march to the sea on the advice of Grant. On November 8, Lincoln is re-elected to the

Presidency defeating Democratic nominee General George B. McClellan. On December 22, Sherman captures the city of Savannah and tells Lincoln it is an early Christmas gift.

1865. Lincoln seeks and gains Democratic support in House for resolution proposing the Thirteenth Amendment to abolish slavery to the states for ratification. (The amendment had been approved by the Senate in April of 1864.) On January 31, the House passes the resolution by a margin of three votes. On March 4, Lincoln delivers his second Inaugural Address. On April 9, the Civil War ends with the surrender of General Lee's Army of Northern Virginia to General Grant at Appomattox Court House in Virginia. On April 10, celebrations break out in Washington. On April 11, Lincoln makes his last public speech dealing mainly with the issues of reconstruction. On April 14, Lincoln is shot in the head by John Wilkes Booth while attending a performance of *Our American Cousin* in Ford's Theatre. Lincoln dies in a nearby boarding house without regaining consciousness at 7:22 in the morning of April 15. On April 19, there is a funeral service in the White House. The Funeral Train departs carrying Lincoln's remains along with those of Willie Lincoln and begins the twelve-day journey back to Springfield, Illinois, and is viewed by millions of people along the way. Lincolns' remains were interred at Oak Ridge Cemetery outside of Springfield. On December 6, the Thirteenth Amendment to the Constitution is finally ratified and slavery is abolished.